This book belongs to:

_____

and, here begins

her journey to Becoming!

Let's go...

To: Wendy —   8/10/21

Welcome to the Art &
Journey of Becoming. This
will be the best season of
your life. Your eyes have
not seen, nor your ears heard
or your heart imagined what
God still has in store for you.
It is my prayer that this
daily devotional will uncover
hidden treasures in your life.
Through your discoveries you
may experience these treasure
bringing indescribable joy &
freedom, love and peace as
you take the journey to
Becoming More!

                    Peace & Blessings
                    Michele D.

MICHELE DECAUL

THE ART OF
Becoming

A 30-Day Devotional & Journal for
Women of Faith Who Desire to Grow

Cover photo credit:
Stacy Pierce

Editor:
Glenda Wright

Interior Layout & Design:
Tarsha L. Campbell

Cover Art Design:
Sherilyn Bennett
Camden Lane Creative Agency
www.camdenlanecreative.com

Published by:
DOMINIONHOUSE Publishing & Design, LLC
P.O. Box 681938 | Orlando, Florida 32868 | 407.703.4800
www.mydominionhouse.com

The Lord gave the Word: great was the company
of those who published it. (Psalms 68:11)

*****

Scripture quotations marked (BSB) are taken from The Holy Bible, Berean Study Bible, BSB Copyright ©2016, 2018 by Bible Hub. Used by Permission. All Rights Reserved Worldwide.

Scripture quotations marked (ESV) are taken from The Holy Bible, English Standard Version® (ESV®), copyright © 2001 by Crossway, a publishing ministry of Good News Publishers. Used by permission. All rights reserved.

"If you don't like where you are,

chose to grow and become."

-Michele DeCaul

TABLE OF CONTENTS

TABLE OF CONTENTS

TABLE OF CONTENTS

"I challenge and encourage you

to take a personal inventory of your life.

Assess where you need to heal,

learn and grow to accomplish your goals

and make an impact."

Becoming:
ARE YOU READY FOR THE JOURNEY?

Not any journey, but a 30-day prayer journey.

For 30 days, our theme will be "BECOME." The word become means "the process of moving from one state to another by actively receiving new information, perspectives, and/or insight; moving, expanding, and emerging into more; awakening and sobering up to the reality of your awesomeness and all that is available to you; making a decision not to settle!"

This theme is designed to anchor you in your identity, so you are strong and ready to receive the increase that is coming your way!

Each day, I will provide scriptures for you to meditate on and focus on in prayer. In your time of prayer, allow God to speak to you about the areas He wants you to grow and evolve in. I believe where you are in your life right now is a temporary position. Who you are right now is a launching pad that is designed to catapult you into greatness, if you allow yourself to become in this season. You must be willing to ask yourself, "What areas does God desire that I grow in? In what areas can I become better?" When you become more like Christ, who is our example, you will, in turn, expand your identity and your capacity.

I challenge and encourage you to take personal inventory of your life. Assess what you need to do, heal from, learn, grow in, or even unlearn in order to accomplish your goals and make an impact. What are the things that are standing in the way of you becoming the best version of yourself? What action steps need to be taken in order for you to become healthy, wise, compassionate, purposeful, loving, and peaceful?

Whatever you need to become, I encourage you to initiate change in your life through prayer. Having a strong spiritual foundation positions you to excel as you transition into the highest version of yourself. When you submit to God first, all other things will fall into place!

"You can't go back to change

the beginning, but you can start

where you are

and change your ending."

-T. S. Lewis

"Each day is a gift that is given, so you can

unwrap your potential, value, significance,

strength, creativity, courage, confidence,

and more. When we build on the

proper foundation, we can expect

greater from our lives."

DAY

1

Becoming:

LAYING THE FOUNDATION

Today, we begin by laying the scriptural foundation for our journey. When you journey through life experiences, you never depart without Him! Why? Because He sees and knows all things. When we approach life with an attitude of not knowing everything, we leave room for God to teach and lead us in the way we should go in order to become!

You were made in the image of God, created and purposed to live your life to the fullest. He gave you His qualities, so you would not be defeated by doubt, worry, shame, low self-esteem, etc. When the foundation has been set (in your mind) and you believe, it prevents excuses, lies, criticisms, and others' opinions from stopping you!

Each day is a gift that is given, so you can unwrap your potential, value, significance, strength, creativity, courage, confidence, and more. When we build on the proper foundation, we can expect greater from our lives. When we build on the proper foundation, we can start before we stop. When we build on the proper foundation, we can go through any storm, challenge, or obstacle with an unapologetic and unstoppable attitude.

God gave us a living example in His son, Jesus Christ, of how to manage our relationships, emotions, enemies, and obstacles while experiencing abundance, freedom, and power. Since we are created in the image of God, we, too, can walk in the same creative power!

Besides, when you know that you belong to God, you can only expect greater in your life. So, let's begin the journey by committing to becoming who you are designed to be.

When you believe, you will BECOME!

Scriptures for prayer, meditation, and journaling your thoughts

•••••

"So God created human beings in his own image. In the image of God he created them; male and female he created them" (Genesis 1:27, NLT).

_____

_____

_____

_____

_____

"For God knew his people in advance, and he chose them to become like his Son, so that his Son would be the firstborn among many brothers and sisters" (Romans 8:29, NLT).

_____

_____

_____

_____

_____

"Shouldn't we expect far greater glory under the new way, now that the Holy Spirit is giving life?" (2 Corinthians 3:8, NLT).

_____

_____

_____

_____

_____

"Dear friends, we are already God's children, but he has not yet shown us what we will be like when Christ appears. But we do know that we will be like him, for we will see him as he really is" (1 John 3:2, NLT).

_____

_____

_____

_____

_____

"Choose to close doors when they are no longer leading you anywhere."

-Michele DeCaul

"You must maintain a Godly mindset by remembering that God has a plan to prosper you, and the blessings that He has prepared for you are bigger than you can imagine."

DAY

2

BECOME!

This is not a casual request but rather an emphatic command.

Say it with me: "Become!"

When God speaks, He doesn't speak to tickle your ears or pump you up like a balloon filled with helium. He speaks because He sees the value of your future and the impact it will make on the world around you.

It is critical that you evolve. People are designed to experience change. Becoming is all about transformation. In life, there are situations that inadvertently shape our beliefs, our values, and even our identities. It's so important to possess the willpower to pursue personal greatness despite the situations you find yourself in. When you are faced with a challenge, do you become consumed with fear, worry, or anxiety, or do you activate your faith and decide to learn a lesson from whatever you can derive from the situation? You must maintain a Godly mindset by remembering that God has a plan to prosper you, and the blessings that He has prepared for you are bigger than you can imagine. That's why the attacks are so great.

I want you to meditate on the scriptures below. Don't be consumed by your fears but be empowered by your faith.

As you read and meditate on the scriptures, take a moment to reflect and then affirm what the Word of God declares in your life.

Scriptures for prayer, meditation,
and journaling your thoughts

•••••

"But it is written, Eye has not seen, nor ear heard, nor has it entered into the heart of man the things which God has prepared for those who love Him" (1 Corinthians 2:9, NKJV).

_____

_____

_____

_____

_____

"For I know the plans I have for you," says the Lord. "They are plans for good and not for disaster, to give you a future and a hope" (Jeremiah 29:11, NLT).

_____

_____

_____

_____

_____

"Many, O Lord my God, are Your wonderful works which You have done and Your thoughts toward us cannot be recounted to You in order; If I would declare and think of them, they are more than can be numbered" (Psalm 40:5, NKJV).

_____

_____

_____

_____

_____

Set your foundation on God's Word, and you will become what He has called you to be and do what He called you to do. Your future is great!

"For I AM taking you from one state of being to another. I AM changing, expanding, cultivating, shaping, and establishing your character to receive ALL that I have for you! I AM doing away with the old so that you can see the masterpiece that I have created within you."

Becoming Affirmations

My ability to conquer

my challenges is limitless;

my potential to succeed

is infinite.

"When you receive God's love, you become

aware and intimately connected to the

things God does in your life."

DAY

3

Become WELL-LOVED

G od wants to take you higher in His love.

You may find yourself surrounded by the love and support of family and friends, or maybe you find that you don't have as much support as you desire. What I know for sure is when God is ready to bless your life, He is not concerned with who will support you or not. You shouldn't worry about it either. When God is for you, no one can stand against you. God's love is enough to fill any and every void. His grace is sufficient to replenish any area where you may lack.

There is no love that can be compared to the love God gives us. There is no striving, doubt, worry, insecurities, or fear in His love. When we reach for God's love, we become well-loved.

For who on earth has the capacity to love us more than the One who created us and sent His only begotten son on to earth to redeem us?

Our lives can only be anchored in the soil of God's love! So, rest in the love of our Heavenly Father. His love is everlasting and eternal. He will never leave you based on the choices you make. His love for you is steadfast, unconditional, and limitless. There is absolutely nothing that can separate you from His love. It's His love that gives us life each day. It's His love that causes us to conquer and be triumphant in every situation. His love creates change in our hearts.

You are not truly anchored if you don't receive God's love. When you receive His love in your life, you can move through pain, move through your fears, move past the opinions of your critics, and move pass your emotions to accomplish the desires of your heart.

When you receive God's love, you become aware and intimately connected to the things God does in your life. Your day begins with Him the moment your eyes open. Oxygen flows through your lungs, sight is given for your day and dreams, and hearing is clearly delivered for relationships and your faith. Predestined purpose is in place for your future, you receive freedom through His principles, healing for your illness, and strength for weariness. Creativity replaces your boredom, hope overtakes your disappointments, finances are delivered for your daily living, peace overcomes your fears, and victory stamps out defeat. And this is just to name a few. You are well-loved!

When you are well-loved, you experience His love internally (heart), then externally.

So, as you remain in the confidence of God's love, you will achieve the desires of your heart.

Scriptures for prayer, meditation, and journaling your thoughts
•••••

"And we have known and believed the love that God has for us. God is love, and he who abides in love abides in God, and God in him" (1 John 4:16, NKJV).

_____

_____

_____

_____

_____

_____

"We love because he first loved us" (1 John 4:19, NKJV).

_____

_____

_____

_____

_____

_____

"And I am convinced that nothing can ever separate us from God's love. Neither death nor life, neither angels nor demons, neither our fears for today nor our worries about tomorrow—not even the powers of hell can separate us from God's love" (Romans 8:38, NLT).

_____

_____

_____

_____

_____

Now, let's think back on a time in your life that you felt loved or even favored by God.

Can you remember praying for something that you feel you didn't necessarily deserve and then received it?

_____

_____

_____

_____

_____

Can you count the number of ways you're well-loved by God daily?

_____

_____

_____

_____

_____

_____

_____

Have you ever needed something in your life and then received it in an unexpected way? If so, explain.

_____

_____

_____

_____

_____

_____

_____

Have you ever felt blessed, covered, or protected? When you reflect on those moments, did it feel like you were loved?

_____

_____

_____

_____

_____

_____

_____

God shows us His love in many different ways. Write out your most memorable encounters that displayed God's love for you.

_____

_____

_____

_____

_____

_____

I AM WELL–LOVED!

"Being patient surrenders you to a process,

and the process is designed to develop,

mature, and cultivate who you

are from within."

DAY

4

Become PATIENT

We live in a society where being patient is not the norm. We can sometimes conform and submit to the "microwave" process.

We can become impatient with ourselves, our careers, jobs, relationships, goals, and even our accomplishments. We can get frustrated or discouraged when things don't happen within our expected timeframe. We may then begin to make moves in haste. Our fear of failure, coupled with our inability to wait, can cause us to do things according to our own will and not God's will.

God is in the business of blessing you, but one key ingredient to your success is that you become patient! Patience is definitely a virtue that is necessary as you navigate through your life or growth process.

Being patient surrenders you to a process, and the process is designed to develop, mature, and cultivate who you are from within.

When you become patient, it removes routines, habits, and cycles from your life.

When you become patient with yourself, you remove unnecessary pressures.

When you become patient, you allow yourself to see your situation from a different perspective.

When you become patient, it expands your maturity and trust in God.

When you become patient, you can arrive at a solution or strategy faster.

When you become patient, you open yourself up to forgiveness.

When you become patient, you give yourself access to wisdom.

While you may be looking for immediate results or rewards, understand that your reward will be released to you during your process of becoming the person who is patient enough to wait on God's best.

Since we know patience is a virtue, like most things that make us better, becoming patient is going to require some practice.

Here are a few techniques that you can implement right away to help you develop more patience in your life.

1. Change your perspective – How can you see things from God's view and not your view? Changing your perspective will slow you down, so you will not become easily angered or irrational.

2. Bite your tongue – Don't always look to respond back to the opinions given by others. Wisdom can rise in silence. When you choose to be silent and hold your opinion, you allow God to give you His wisdom concerning the matter.

3. Give up the right to be right – You don't always have to have the last word. You don't always have to act like you have all the right answers. Sometimes, you will be wrong, so give up the right to be right so that you can listen to your heart and not others' opinions.

Scriptures for prayer, meditation, and journaling your thoughts

•••••

"Love is patient, love is kind. It does not envy, it does not boast, it is not proud" (1 Corinthians 13:4, NIV).

Are you patient with yourself and others? If not, in what ways can you become more patient with yourself? Identify one or two relationships and share ways you can become more patient.

_____

_____

_____

_____

_____

"Whoever is patient has great understanding, but one who is quick-tempered displays folly" (Proverbs 14:29, NIV).

In what areas of your life are you frustrated, quick-tempered, or angry? How can being patient help you gain greater understanding?

_____

_____

_____

_____

_____

_____

_____

"The Lord is not slow in keeping his promise, as some understand slowness. Instead He is patient with you, not wanting anyone to perish, but everyone to come to repentance" (2 Peter 3:9, NIV).

_____

_____

_____

_____

Taking responsibility for your actions is one step in helping you slow down before reacting. What behaviors will you become responsible for changing and not doing again?

_____

_____

_____

_____

Do you allow your emotions to manipulate you to become unforgiving, irrational, or angry? When was the last time you gained power over your emotions and resisted the urge to respond in anger?

_____

_____

_____

_____

_____

Becoming patient is your invitation to a well-managed life!

I AM PATIENT!

Becoming Affirmations

I respect my limitations

and thank myself for the things

I am able to accomplish.

"Your journey is designed for greatness
and not comfort. Vulnerability is the
birthplace of greater connection of self,
deeper awareness, courage,
empathy, and creativity."

DAY

5

Become VULNERABLE

I t's easy to fall prey to the boundaries of your comfort zone. It is easy to fall prey to your emotions. It is easy to fall prey to your own story. It is easy to fall prey to remaining silent or hidden. It is easy to fall prey to past pain. It is also easy to fall prey to being a victim. Being a woman, it is sometimes easy to move through life withdrawn, introverted, uncommunicative, shy, restrained, and even quiet; however, doing so can be quite limiting.

Life changes, a new job, health concerns, a job promotion, divorce, entrepreneurship, loss of a loved one, a broken relationship, loss of a job, having a baby, getting married, and other experiences can bring highs and lows in our lives. Through these personalized changes, it's easy to become withdrawn or emotionally lost. When you don't manage and become aware of your emotions, you can risk living your life in silence!

When you become vulnerable, it boosts your ability to acknowledge and consider how you feel. With vulnerability, it can be scary at times because there is an uncertainty with your emotions along with the risk of being emotionally exposed. When you become vulnerable, you don't cover up and hide, but you express how you feel despite how others may feel or what they may say. It's moving in faith and trusting that God is with you. Your journey is designed for greatness, and not comfort. Vulnerability is the birthplace of greater connection of self, deeper awareness, courage, empathy, and creativity.

Being vulnerable strips you of your controls, your fears, your sabotaging thoughts, others' opinions, and the voices of your critics, and it pushes you into freedom, creativity, self-expression, possibilities. Most importantly, it pushes you closer to your purpose and dreams.

I can remember times where vulnerability showed up unplanned and unscripted. I was doing a Facebook Live one morning—and please note that I had been doing it for about two years at the time. However, during this time, I was transitioning roles at my church, and the experience was bittersweet. Well, this particular morning, I started off as my "happy-go-lucky self" with my pre-planned topic in mind. But all of sudden, I made a statement that hit me so deeply I couldn't find my way back or stop my thoughts from spinning out of control. In that moment, I remembered the five years of sacrifices, hard work, opposition, celebrations, dedication, building, teamwork, and so much more. I was a weeping ball of mess on Facebook! When I ended the session, I was so embarrassed I wanted to delete it because I'd cried and shared my heart so publicly.

After I moved through my emotional mush of feelings of judgement, criticism, rejection, and indifference and made it to the other side, I appreciated my unscripted expression, courage, and strength. I didn't have time to think about what others would say or think because vulnerability pushed me into greater self-awareness and greater emotional strength. Rather than running or deleting the video, I worked my way through it to see my own strength. Vulnerability increases your strength, as it detaches you from others' criticisms, opinions, and expectations.

Don't allow yourself to forget that you're strong and you can handle this.

Scriptures for prayer, meditation, and journaling your thoughts

•••••

"I can do all things through him who strengthens me" (Philippians 4:13, NKJV).

_____

_____

_____

_____

_____

"Trust in the Lord with all your heart, and lean not on your own understanding. In all your ways acknowledge him, and He shall direct your paths" (Proverbs 3:5-6, NKJV).

_____

_____

_____

_____

_____

"If any of you lack wisdom, let him ask God, who gives to all liberally without reproach, and it will be given to him. But let him ask in faith, with no doubting, for he who doubts is like a wave of the sea driven and tossed by the wind. For let not that man suppose that he will receive anything from the Lord" (James 1:5-7, NKJV).

_____

_____

_____

_____

_____

_____

Vulnerability says let's move in freedom, courage, and strength. So, let's take a few steps together.

Love and appreciate you first. When you believe you are worthy of love and belonging, you open yourself to becoming more vulnerable. Let yourself know how many ways you love and appreciate you.

_____

_____

_____

_____

_____

The knee jerk reaction. Stay in tune with your emotions and don't resist. When you are on the brink of your feelings coming to the surface, don't pull back; take note and write them down. Train yourself to stop and listen to your heart. Think of an experience that brought about some emotions, then stop and listen to your heart. Now write down how you feel.

_____

_____

_____

_____

_____

Share your heart! Open your heart to someone you trust. Write down a vulnerable moment below, and express feelings, failures, and thoughts. Then share! This will give you practice, courage, and strength.

_____

_____

_____

_____

_____

I AM VULNERABLE!

Becoming Affirmations

I love myself

My best self is emerging every day.

I have all that I need

to make today a great day.

I am worthy of love and endless joy.

I choose to STOP apologizing

for being me.

"Selfless living is a sign of a forgiving and

pure heart. When you are selfless, your

motive is to help, support,

inspire, encourage, and empower

those around you."

DAY
6

Become
SELFLESS

Selfless means having no regard of self or being unselfish.

As we journey through life, it is easy to lose our way doing things because of our own selfish ways and desires. Having selfish desires and only thinking about me, myself, and I is a very limited way of living your life. I know you didn't get this way overnight; it was the many experiences and pains of life that probably got you fed up with people and life. When the people you're in relationships with don't value you, it's easy to isolate yourself and guard your heart. Over time, you can become unforgiving, bitter, angry, and depressed. These feelings will also convince you to never trust anyone ever again because they are going to hurt you like the last person. But we don't realize that this position will cause us to become guarded and selfish. When you become selfish, you will also have the tendency to become controlling; you will attempt to control others or the situation, so you don't experience any further pain.

This type of living limits the ways God wants to bless you. Selfish behaviors or tendencies block God from fixing the broken pieces of your heart. When your heart is broken, it is difficult to trust anyone, including yourself, others, and even God.

Selfishness will not only block God from fixing your situation, but it will also block you from getting closer to Him.

From the very beginning of time, God created human beings with the intent to connect and to have a sense of belonging. Selfishness creates isolation, greed, dissension, separation, a self-made mentality, disconnection, and disunity in relationships.

You see, the power of being selfless is designed to create powerful relationships. Selfless living is a sign of a forgiving and pure heart. When you are selfless, your motive is to help, support, inspire, encourage, and empower those around you. These are some of the essential components of bringing unity, harmony, connection, creativity, and productivity into relationships. We can't achieve greatness on our own; it has been designed to happen in relationships! When you operate in a selfless mentality, it provides access for others to bless you with their time, ideas, support, encouragement, money, and resources for your next level.

Living selflessly begins with looking at your heart and not allowing any negative emotions to consume or change you into a selfish person.

Here's what's great: if you have found yourself being selfish a time or two in the past or yesterday, no worries. Here is your invitation to change or, rather, to become.

You now have the permission to become different. Choose to be different because you understand that selfishness will only get you out of position from receiving your best. However, living selflessly will position you for opportunities that will blow your mind!

The key ingredient to moving from selfishness to selflessness is forgiveness.

Scriptures for prayer, meditation, and journaling your thoughts

•••••

"The second is this: 'Love your neighbor as yourself.' There is no commandment greater than these" (Mark 12:31, NIV).

_____

_____

_____

_____

_____

_____

"Finally, all of you, have unity of mind, sympathy, brotherly love, a tender heart, and a humble mind" (1 Peter 3:8, ESV).

_____

_____

_____

_____

_____

_____

"Forget about the wrong things people do to you. And do not try to get even. Love your neighbor as you love yourself. I am the Lord" (Leviticus 19:18, NCV).

_____

_____

_____

_____

_____

_____

"Instead of being motivated by selfish ambition or vanity, each of you should, in humility, be moved to treat one another as more important than yourself. Each of you should be concerned not only about your own interests, but about the interests of others as well" (Philippians 2:3-4, NET).

_____

_____

_____

_____

_____

_____

Now that you have read the scriptures, let's take action! Make a list of the people you want to forgive and complete the following statements. Fill in the blank with their names and what they did to cause the pain. This action is not about them, but it is all about you rising up to become selfless. If you need additional blank statements, feel free to use additional paper.

I forgive _____ for_____.

I forgive _____ for_____.

I forgive _____ for_____.

I forgive _____ for_____.

I forgive _____ for_____.

I forgive _____ for_____.

I forgive _____ for_____.

I forgive _____ for_____.

Let's pray. . .

Father, we thank you for your love, grace, and mercy. Today, I want to become selfless. I thank You for the process and strategy of forgiving others who have hurt me in my past. Your Word declares that I should hold nothing in my heart against anyone, and I am to love my neighbor as myself. Since you were faithful to forgive me for my wrongdoings, give me the strength and courage to forgive others for what they did to me. I also pray a special prayer to forgive myself for all of my actions, thoughts, and behaviors that were selfish. I desire to become selfless, and I know You will help me to rise up and become. In Jesus' name I pray. Amen.

I AM SELFLESS!

"Being who you are not, or apologizing for who you are, will only frustrate you and lead you miles away from your uniqueness, your peace, and your purpose."

DAY

7

Become UNAPOLOGETICALLY YOU

I am sorry. I am sorry. I am sorry.

Have you ever found yourself continuously apologizing for who you are or maybe for some of the things you have done? There is nothing wrong with apologizing; however, if you continue reliving that experience over and over, it will keep you emotionally drained and taking on a mindset of a victim.

I can remember times that I apologized to people for things that really didn't need an apology. Because of my insecurities, I would say things like "I'm sorry I didn't have the answer. I'm sorry that I failed the test. I'm sorry I wasn't able to get to the phone. I'm sorry that I am not dressed for the occasion. I'm sorry I didn't know." By apologizing, I thought those around me would accept me and not reject me.

The truth is: making apologies based on insecurities doesn't work.

From today forward, no more apologizing for who you are. We all go through different experiences in life; however, those experiences should not dictate, validate, or qualify your existence. We have a way of finding a way to lower our standards to fit into society's view or others' views or expectations of who they think we are.

How easy is it to be someone else? EASY... It is extremely easy to copy someone's mannerisms, clothing, and style. It's easy to compromise who you are, share the same opinion as others, and neglect yourself. It's easy, physically easy, but emotionally frustrating because you are denying who you are. It's easy to hide and not discover the wonderful workmanship you are. In this season, there will be no more living in the shadows of who you were created to be.

You were created uniquely, which means your responses, ideas, and opinions will be different at times. Therefore, stop working overtime trying to fit in or trying to be the same as others! Being who you are not, or apologizing for who you are, will only frustrate you and lead you miles away from your uniqueness, your peace, and your purpose. What you bring to the world is valuable and requires you to bring it.

Start picking out the good things about yourself, rather than the imperfections. Be yourself. Don't be afraid to like something, to wear something, or to do something you like. Don't make apologies for things that make you happy. Don't apologize for being yourself. Be who you are, fearlessly and unapologetically.

Let's go!

List 10 things you absolutely love about you.

1. _____

2. _____

3. _____

4. _____

5. _____

6. _____

7. _____

8. _____

9. _____

10. _____

Now, celebrate unapologetically!

Scriptures for prayer, meditation, and journaling your thoughts

•••••

"I will praise you; for I am fearfully and wonderfully made: Marvelous are your works; And that my soul knows right well" (Psalm 139:14, NKJV).

_____

_____

_____

_____

_____

You are a marvelous work of His. He made you to be unique in this world, to bring to it something that it hasn't had before. He made you the way you are. Why would you try to change yourself when He worked so hard on all the little details of who you are?

_____

_____

_____

_____

_____

"For we are God's masterpiece. He has created us anew in Christ Jesus, so we can do the good things he planned for us long ago" (Ephesians 2:10, NLT).

_____

_____

_____

_____

_____

You are one of a kind! So why be more like everyone else? You may think you are weird, strange, unlovable, or unwanted the way you are, but you are not. There is always someone striving to be like you because of what they see in you.

_____

_____

_____

_____

_____

_____

_____

Every ounce of your life is a workmanship, so never apologize for who you are and what you went through because you have been created wonderfully and fearfully!

_____

_____

_____

_____

_____

_____

I AM UNAPOLOGETICALLY ME!

Becoming Affirmations

I am a beautiful person from within.

I am beautiful and I am worthy of every

beautiful thing in this world.

I am beautifully confident.

"When you operate in joy, you leave no

room for your critics or any negative

thoughts to hinder, manipulate, change,

or cause you to respond

in a way that you lose control. "

DAY
8

Become
JOYFUL

To become joyful simply means to have an expression of joy. It is the passion or emotion that produces excitement, exhilaration, gladness, jubilance, and exuberance.

To be joyful is a state of being that originates from thoughts. You have the power and permission to choose joy at any time. God clearly lets us know He has given us joy, so we can have strength through any experience we go through.

What do you allow to steal your joy? If joy can be stolen, that means joy can be selected!

To become joyful means you must choose joy. How do you choose joy? Glad you asked. Choosing joy requires your active participation, no matter the situation. When disappointments arise, you still have the option to choose joy. I remember doing my yearly annual woman's exam one particular season. However, this time, the exam went a little differently than I expected.

When the doctor examined my breasts, she stated that she felt a small lump in one of my breasts and recommended that I get a mammogram. Even though it wasn't my first time getting a mammogram, this time felt different. Immediately, the death sentence of cancer started creating stories in my head. My thoughts started closing the chapter on my life. When I realized I was giving permission for death to enter my life through my thoughts, I had to shake off these feelings, so I could choose differently. I had to reach beyond my feelings into joy.

Reaching beyond where you are will require you to meditate and believe the promises and plans of God for your life. When you meditate on what brings you joy, it changes the outcome of your thoughts. The question is: when life is not going your way, do you have the ability to choose thoughts that can bring you joy? Do you have reasons why you should be joyful? If you're breathing and reading this message, the answer is yes!

When you operate in joy, you leave no room for your critics or any negative thoughts to hinder, manipulate, change, or cause you to respond in a way that you lose control. Joy, instead, will produce patience, peace, and faith because you understand who is in control.

Joy is your strength, and when you choose it, you will win every battle and confuse your critics! When joy becomes your thermostat, you set the temperature when you go through various life experiences. Can I tell you that the strength of joy gave me peace when the results of my mammogram were negative?

Joy is a choice, so let's choose to discover some things that bring joy in our lives.

List five things that bring joy to your life.

1. _____
2. _____
3. _____
4. _____
5. _____

List five promises of God that bring joy to your life.

1. _____
2. _____
3. _____
4. _____
5. _____

Scriptures for prayer, meditation,
and journaling your thoughts
•••••

"Though you have not seen him, you love him; and even though you do not see him now, you believe in him and are filled with an inexpressible and glorious joy" (1 Peter 1:8, NIV).

_____

_____

_____

_____

_____

"Be joyful in hope, patient in affliction, faithful in prayer" (Romans 12:12, NIV).

_____

_____

_____

_____

_____

_____

". . . Do not grieve, for the joy of the Lord is your strength" (Nehemiah 8:10, NIV).

_____

_____

_____

_____

_____

_____

I AM JOYFUL!

"Resilience is a form of mental training and stamina. God wants you to look beyond the bad and see His principles and promises for your life."

DAY
9

Become
RESILIENT

Are you maintaining your course on this devotional journey? Whatever you do, don't give up—keep pressing on this journey because there is something great at the end. Okay, let's go.

I have some great news for you. You are not exempt from having challenges or trials. Yes, you heard me correctly. You are not exempt! How would you examine the depth of your potential strength or wisdom if you didn't have opposing situations to face? In those moments, how would you respond? Are you the type of person to complain, give up, give in, avoid, or run from the situation? What experiences have caused you to run in fear? What experiences have kept you away from your purpose?

I remember I was in a new position, and the team that I had inherited had individuals who were excited about my leadership, but then there were others who weren't excited. Even though it was only two people, those two individuals attempted to poison the others with their views and opinions, while falsely showing their support for me. These two individuals challenged and undermined my authority whenever they saw an opportunity.

Everything in me wanted to walk away from the position to protect my feelings and my character. Their display of sabotaging tactics left me feeling as though I wasn't good enough for the role and I began to doubt my skills, abilities, and expertise.

I realized my fight was not to fight with them, but my fight was to remain in position, focusing on my responsibilities and not on them. I redirected my focus, and it changed my perspective and drive to become resilient!

Do you know that who I am was birthed in resilience? If I didn't have challenges, obstacles, and opposition, I would have nothing to cultivate my potential. My potential, like yours, is being birthed in the cocoon of resilience.

When your opposition, challenges, and trials look like they are defeating you, what is actually happening is the development of solutions, new insight, revelation, and discoveries.

How you respond in tough times determines your mental strength and emotional stability. Resilience is a form of mental training and stamina. God wants you to look beyond the bad and see His principles and promises for your life. The resilient know how to look past the circumstance and into the mind of Christ to seek peace and determine their response.

Let's measure the level of your resilience.

Despite what is going on in your life, do you still have the capacity to treat others with respect, understanding, and compassion?

When you have experienced a failure, are you willing to be brave and try again?

When times are challenging, are you able to not take life so seriously but laugh during the difficult times?

Do you allow your past experiences and tragedies to define your identity?

When you make a mistake, do you take responsibility for your choices?

When something bad happens, are you able to find understanding and move forward?

If you answered yes to four or more of these questions, you have a strong measure of resilience!

Scriptures for prayer, meditation, and journaling your thoughts

•••••

The resilient give God honor in every situation.

"Then Job arose, tore his robe, and shaved his head; and he fell to the ground and worshiped. And he said: "Naked I came from my mother's womb, And naked shall I return there. The Lord gave, and the Lord has taken away; Blessed be the name of the Lord" (Job 1:20-21, NKJV).

In what ways do you honor God for the moments in life you were resilient?

_____

_____

_____

_____

_____

The resilient know every trial produces a win.

"Consider it pure joy, my brothers, when you are involved in various trials, because you know that the testing of your faith produces endurance. But you must let endurance have its full effect, so that you may be mature and complete, lacking nothing" (James 1:2-4, NIV).

Now that you have experienced wins, list some of the wins you have experienced.

_____

_____

_____

_____

_____

The resilient bounce back and keep moving.

"We are troubled on every side, yet not distressed; we are perplexed, but not in despair; Persecuted, but not forsaken; cast down, but not destroyed" (2 Corinthians 4:8-9, KJV).

"The righteous keep moving forward, and those with clean hands become stronger and stronger" (Job 17:9, NLT).

List the ways you keep it moving.

_____

_____

_____

_____

_____

The resilient focus their attention on God.

"We must focus on Jesus, the source and goal of our faith. He saw the joy ahead of him, so he endured death on the cross and ignored the disgrace it brought him. Then he received the highest position in heaven, the one next to the throne of God. Think about Jesus, who endured opposition from sinners, so that you don't become tired and give up" (Hebrews 12:2-3, GWS).

What are you currently focused on? How does it impact your resilience?

_____

_____

_____

_____

_____

The resilient trust God and not themselves.

"Trust in the Lord with all your heart and lean not on your own understanding. In all your ways submit to Him, and he will make your paths straight" (Proverbs 3:5-6, NIV).

Where does your trust lie? Is it in your friends, family members, spouse, or boss? If so, how does that impact your resilience?

_____

_____

_____

_____

_____

The resilient pray in the time of trouble.

"Don't worry about anything; instead pray about everything. Tell God what you need and thank him for all he has done. Then you will experience God's peace, which exceeds anything we can understand. His peace will guard your hearts and minds as you live in Christ Jesus" (Philippians 4:6-7, NLT).
"Pray to me when you are in trouble. I will deliver you, and you will honor me" (Psalm 50:15, NET).

What impact does your prayer life have on your resilience?

_____

_____

_____

_____

_____

We remain resilient because we know God has a plan for us.

"For I know the thoughts that I think toward you, saith the LORD, thoughts of peace, and not of evil, to give you an expected end" (Jeremiah 29:11, KJV).

When you know, your resilience is a guarantee. So, what do you know about your future?

_____

_____

_____

_____

_____

I AM RESILIENT!

Becoming
Affirmations

I believe in myself.

I am at peace with my body and accept it as

it is, because it was created to do

amazing things.

I love and respect my body and I take care

of it through speaking positively,

eating healthily and exercising.

I am responsible for what happens to my

body, so I treat it with love, respect,

care and honor.

"The problem with wavering is that it is designed to exhaust you and keep you in limbo. It will make you so tired that it prevents you from hearing God and making the correct decisions for your life."

DAY
10

Become
STEADFAST

B ecome steadfast in making your decisions.
Do you ever find yourself wavering between decisions? What problems cause doubt? What experience has crippled you with worry? Do you fear making certain decisions?

If you were honest and said "yes" to any of these questions, you have traveled through or are currently in a place of uncertainty when it comes to going out to eat, career changes, job changes, what to wear, hanging out with friends, being in a relationship, or even ending a relationship. You may have even questioned being in a relationship with God and your level of faith to believe. Living in a place of uncertainty prevents you from living at your personal best!

My teenage daughter is prone to this. In the morning, when she is getting dressed for school, she will take out 10 outfits and 10 combinations (exaggerating) and is confused and wants my input. Even when I give her my suggestions, she still changes her mind. She is very indecisive in various areas of her life. I know you probably are able to relate to this example when it comes to making certain decisions in your life. Should I go out with him? Should I take the job? Should I apply for the promotion? Should I go back to school? Should I take a vacation at this time? Should I go to the doctor? The list goes on and on.

The problem with wavering is that it is designed to exhaust you and keep you in limbo. It will make you so tired that it prevents you from hearing God and making the correct decisions for your life. There are some cases in which wavering will completely stop you from making a decision, resulting in you putting your life on hold (with feelings of being stuck). When you waver in your thoughts, it keeps your life in limbo and confusion, and it makes it makes you dependent on others. When you are unable to make a decision, you place control of your life in the hands of others.

When we waver, it is a sign that we have allowed our emotions to sit in the driver's seat of our lives. Our emotions have no directions, no desire to stop, and no clue where to go. Living in a place of uncertainty allows your life to be a revolving door that others can enter and exit without permission.

God didn't design you to be in a place of limbo. You have been created in power and in purpose. Your life has already been orchestrated and planned, with your steps already being ordered. When we understand that our lives have been planned and purposed, it helps to eliminate worry, doubt, indecisiveness, wavering, and uncertainty. You are not a victim. When you position and establish yourself in God, you remain anchored in His promises. At the end of the day, the things you will face will always change, but His principles, promises, and purpose will never change!

Making and taking responsibilities for your decisions prevents others from controlling your life.

Don't become a slave to indecisiveness or the opinions of others. The best thing you can do for yourself when you come to crossroads is make your own decisions. When you make the decision, it becomes your decision. Even if it wasn't the right decision, you get the opportunity to grow your trust and confidence as you make decisions for your life.

Become steadfast, standing firm in God's Word, and you will gain control over your life.

Take your life back!

1. Don't overthink your decisions – Overthinking can stop you before you start. You are not able to predict the outcome of your decision. This is where you have to take ownership of your decision, trust yourself, and be okay with the outcome.

2. Take your time – What is the rush? Plan ahead and take your time. Don't make irrational, impulsive decisions. These types of decisions will have your emotions all over the place, with no direction or goal, because you are pressured by time. Be in control and give yourself time (however, not too much time) to make a decision. Depending on the type of decision, give yourself at least two hours, so you can plan accordingly.

3. What's the worst that can happen? – Ask yourself what is the worst that can happen. If you aren't putting yourself in danger or your decision is not going to end your life or someone else's, you can bounce back from the outcome.

4. Move in fear – We avoid making decisions because we are sometimes afraid, or we are afraid to fail. The truth is: you will never know the outcome if you don't move in the fear. Fear will manipulate you into not trying or making a decision for your life. Don't take the bait. Move with fear and together you will see the outcome for yourself.

5. Think about your previous yes – Take a moment to remember the time you made a decision that was a great choice for you. When you remember the outcome of your great decision, it will give you the confidence you need to make the current decision. Every decision you make is strength and confidence for the next decision.

6. Who are you trying to please? – Take a moment to ask yourself, "Who am I trying to please?" If you are aiming to please someone, you are going to potentially set yourself up to be disappointed. Trying to please others will always make you a moving target because some people are fickle in their emotions and desires.

7. Not perfection, but peace – Strive to have a peace of mind. Having peace is keeping you in control mind, body, and spirit. If you're striving for perfection in your decision, then you are more concerned about how you will look in front of others. Making decisions for others will keep you in limbo and provide you no peace. Stay away from a perfectionistic mindset and seek peace above all else.

**Scriptures for prayer, meditation,
and journaling your thoughts**

•••••

"Let us hold fast the confession of our hope without wavering, for he is faithful that promised" (Hebrews 10:23, KJV).

_____

_____

_____

_____

_____

"Therefore, my beloved brethren, be ye steadfast, unmoveable, always abounding in the work of the Lord, forasmuch as ye know that your labour is not in vain in the Lord" (1 Corinthians 15:58, KJV).

_____

_____

_____

_____

_____

"It is for freedom that Christ has set us free. Stand firm, then, and do not be encumbered once more by a yoke of slavery" (Galatians 5:1, BSB).

_____

_____

_____

_____

_____

"So that we may no longer be children, tossed to and fro by the waves and carried about by every wind of doctrine, by human cunning, by craftiness in deceitful schemes" (Ephesians 4:14, ESV).

_____

_____

_____

_____

_____

I AM STEADFAST!

"Guilt can function one or two ways in your life. When it lingers in your heart too long, it can lead to shame and many other negative emotions that will aid in restricting your future..."

DAY
11

Become
GUILT-FREE

No more guilt about broken/divorced relationships! No more guilt about making yourself a priority! No more guilt about your achievements in life! No more guilt about your education! No more guilt about your career! No more guilt about your past decisions! No more guilt about your children or parenting! No more guilt about your failures! No more guilt about missed opportunities! No more guilt about unmet expectations! No more guilt about a lost loved one! No more guilt about starting over again! No more guilt about your age, gender, or nationality!

Have you ever found yourself saying, "Is there something I could have done differently?" or "Maybe if I said it this way." or "It was my fault everything turned out the way it did!" or "I wish I would have been there for her/him more!" or "But I wasn't there to protect them!"

What is all this guilt about? Guilt is not a nice feeling. It is very unsettling, and if not dealt with through the love of God, it can be damaging. We can sometimes try to avoid it, and when we can't get away from it, we try to get rid of it or put the blame on others or even on ourselves. Guilt can arise from our family, friends, society, religion, or from within us. It can arise consciously and sometimes subconsciously. Guilt can begin in our childhood and continue into our adult lives.

Guilt can function in one or two ways in your life. When it lingers in your heart too long, it can lead to shame and many other negative emotions that will aid in restricting your future. On the contrary, guilt can also be a signal for you to take responsibility for your actions. When we make decisions that are unproductive and harmful to others and even ourselves, guilt can be an alert that something needs to change.

You were not created to carry the weight of guilt. The reason why we are in relationship with Christ is because of His love for us. This is the good news of the gospel of Jesus Christ! God gave His only begotten Son as a gift and a sacrifice of love. Jesus died, He was buried, and then rose from the grave, so we would have freedom. In Him, we are free from all of our sins. In Him, we are free from the guilt brought on by the opinions of man or our past behaviors and choices. The mental and emotional freedom that we experience in Christ is priceless!

Today, God wants you to free your mind. Evict guilt and make space in your mind by renewing and meditating on God's Word. Focus on God's promises concerning your freedom. Make a declaration today that you give yourself permission to release *all* guilt.

Scriptures for prayer, meditation, and journaling your thoughts

•••••

"For God did not send His Son into the world to condemn the world, but that the world through Him might be saved" (John 3:17, NKJV).

It's not God's purpose to condemn you; it's His desire to take away your sins, to keep you from sin, and to save you through Jesus Christ.

_____

_____

_____

_____

_____

_____

"For I will be merciful to their unrighteousness, and their sins and their lawless deeds I will remember no more" (Hebrews 8:12, NKJV).

In His great mercy, God erases your sin from His memory!

_____

_____

"As far as the east is from the west, so far has He removed our transgressions from us" (Psalm 103:12, NIV).

It gives you a wonderful feeling of freedom to be separated from your sins and past and to be joined with God.

"Therefore, if any man be in Christ, he is a new creature; old things are passed away; behold, all things are new" (2 Corinthians 5:17, KJV).

Through salvation, I have been made new.

_____

_____

_____

What are some of the things that you are still holding against your-self? We know that God forgives us daily, so why is it so hard for us to forgive ourselves? Unknowingly, we carry the burden of past experiences that are no longer relevant. Perhaps you don't realize that you are still attached to a mistake.

Take this time to assess. Take inventory of your life. There are things that we all wish we could do differently. What are some of those things in your life?

_____

_____

_____

_____

_____

_____

It's quite normal to have regrets; it's a part of the human experience. The problem is that while it may very well be normal, it is not always healthy.

So, review your list. Your list may reflect what you would do differently if given the chance, but the list is void of all of the many things that you did right, all of the tough decisions you have had to make, and all of the hard times you survived. The reason why God forgives us is because His grace is sufficient to cover every thorn. He already paid the ultimate cost for our condemnation. Give yourself a little more grace, release the past, and embrace the future. What I've learned is that the things of my past in comparison to what God has stored up for me in my future can't be compared. Choose to focus more on where you are. After all, now is all you really have power over. Learn from your past, but then let it go.

I LIVE GUILT FREE!

"Fear has the potential to keep you limited

if you believe the false story. Fear can keep

you away from living the life

that you have dreamed of."

DAY
12

Become
FEARLESS

It is absolutely normal to feel afraid, but it's a choice to accept or be enslaved by it. To live fearlessly is the not living in the absence of fear but rather having a mastery of fear. To live fearlessly is how we respond. Living fearlessly is moving in spite of your fear of falling down and getting back up. The more familiar you become with the outcome, the more fearless you will be and the easier your journey.

You are not designed to live in fear, even though you will experience challenges in life that will trigger fear. There are so many things we can be fearful of – bugs, roller coasters, confrontation, closed spaces, traveling on an airplane, heights, failure, etc. When fear arises, it is important to recognize what it is associated with in your mind. What story are you telling yourself to produce the fear? Is the story you are telling yourself true?

Fear has the potential to keep you limited if you believe the false story. Fear can keep you away from living the life that you have dreamed of. Fear will blind you to seeing the possibilities on the other side.

Recently, I was asked to speak for a millionaire businessman at one of his events. The request was so random that I only had a day or two to decide. Even though he had asked me several times before in conversation, I never took him seriously. However, this time, when the request came, he was serious. In that moment, I screamed, and then fear began to surface in my thoughts. Will his audience receive me? How will I fill his shoes? What will I say? What if no one shows up? What if I don't say the right things? Fear threw so many lies and false expectations at me, I had to say STOP! I released myself from the fear by stating what is actually true.

I smashed and challenged fear with the truth. The TRUTH IS... I was invited to speak; I didn't invite myself. I was invited because of my abilities. I am created to empower and bring life. Whatever I share will be impactful. I am a builder and speak life into the lives of many. When I speak, my voice helps to unlock struggles, blocks, and limitations. I am a doubt dissolver, and I was created to do this. Whether there's one or one thousand people, I will share my best.

Understand that your critics and your inner mean voice's main role is to neutralize you, so you don't move powerfully into your future. Your calling is on the other side of your fears! Stepping into your purpose with the power and authority that is available to you requires your authenticity. You must be willing to embrace and accept who God created you to be. Your identity along with your beliefs play a very big part in this. This is not a call to be perfect but purposeful. When you understand and come in agreement with God, He will fill you with courage, untangle knots of insecurity, and cancel every lie telling you to hide your true self from the world.

When you allow God to fill you, it will create a new space to receive the confidence you need to be yourself, despite what others may think or say. The confidence that you will possess will give you the boldness to move through fear, even when criticism and judgment comes to stand in your way. Even though fear will certainly come from time to time, you will have the grace and strength to go against it and not submit to or become a slave to it.

God designed you to be real with Him, yourself, and others. All that you have gone through—achievements and disappointments— all are a part of your story. Your story is meant to be shared with the world, but it will require your confidence to release it. Deep within those moments are opportunities to share about the saving power of Jesus to those around you. All of this and more exists on the other side of fear.

You were made in love and purpose. Your Heavenly Father delights in your beauty and all that He has created you to be and do in this world. So, no more hiding!

Live the life that will change you and others from the inside out!

Scriptures for prayer, meditation, and journaling your thoughts

•••••

"For God has not given us a spirit of fear, but of power, and of love, and a sound mind" (1 Timothy 1:7, (KJV).

_____

_____

_____

_____

_____

_____

"The LORD is with me; I will not be afraid. What can mere mortals do to me?" (Psalm 118:6, NIV).

_____

_____

_____

_____

_____

"Have I not commanded you? Be strong and courageous. Do not be afraid; do not be discouraged, for the LORD your God will be with you wherever you go" (Joshua 1:9, NIV).

"Even though I walk through the darkest valley, I will fear no evil, for you are with me; your rod and your staff, they comfort me" (Psalm 23:4, NIV).

"I prayed to the LORD, and he answered me; He freed me from all my fears" (Psalm 34:4, NLT).

_____

_____

_____

_____

_____

_____

"The LORD is my light and my salvation; whom shall I fear? The LORD is the strength of my life; of whom shall I be afraid?" (Psalm 27:1, KJV).

_____

_____

_____

_____

_____

_____

I LIVE FEARLESSLY!

"Lies and secrets will keep you in hiding

and will prevent you from living your life

in freedom. The best gift you can

give yourself is to tell the truth

without judging it."

DAY
13

Become
TRUTHFUL

Today, I was reading and meditating on Acts 5:1-10, where Ananias and Sapphira sold a piece of land and then kept some of the money secretly. When confronted by Peter on two separate occasions, they both lied to him, and as a result, they died. Their deaths occurred because they lied to the Holy Spirit!

You see, their deaths were a result of them grieving the Holy Spirit by lying. First, they didn't remember that the Holy Spirit knows all things and loved them with a love that is unfailing. But in the end, they chose the lie over the truth.

How often do we choose the lie over the truth? We can sometimes forget that God sees our thoughts. He says, in Psalm 139:2-3, "You know my thoughts from far away. You know everything I do. You know what I'm going to say before I say it." Ananias and Sapphira lied not only to God but also to themselves.

There are times when we lie to ourselves about ourselves. Our lies can contain an over exaggeration or underestimation of who we are. When we believe our lies, we go through life not being authentically who God has called us to be. When you lie, it grieves the Holy Spirit and causes you to distance yourself from God. When you distance yourself from the supplier of life, there is an experience of loneliness and an emptiness within your soul.

Lies and secrets will keep you in hiding and will prevent you from living your life in freedom. The best gift you can give yourself is to tell the truth without judging it. The lie that Ananias and Sapphira told stemmed from fear, greed, and poverty (thinking they would not have enough). For some, we lie because of the shame, guilt, embarrassment, rejection, low self-worth, pride, and other emotions. We don't want to risk looking a certain way in our relationships with friends, co-workers, family members, spouse, business partners, or employees. Choosing the lie to cover up your choices hides your authenticity.

I remember one of my clients who used makeup to cover up her flaws. She was afraid people would not accept her with the imperfections in her skin. She wouldn't go anywhere without her makeup. Her makeup not only covered her skin's flaws but also limited her from being truly who she was. Her whole life she lived up to the expectations of others.

She lived with secrets for over 40 years, and she thought others could see it. Not until we began coaching and examined the secrets with truth was she able to see that living her life based on secrets produced a life of shame, fear, and guilt. This process allowed her to realize she no longer needed the makeup as a coverup for her imperfections, but she needed to realize that her beauty was really who she is from within.

By understanding that people accepted her because of her inner beauty and not her skin imperfections, she became free, free to work out, grocery shop, and hang out with friends without makeup. No more secrets, no more loneliness, and no more depression or emptiness. She was free from the secrets and now had the ability to wear makeup at her convenience.

When you see the truth behind why you lie, it creates freedom and authenticity. God is so awesome that He built forgiveness, confession, and repentance into His principles of living as opportunities to keep us in truth. Telling the truth will keep you from deception, inauthenticity, and frustration.

Here is your invitation to become truthful.

Are you ready to be truthful and live free? Well, let's go!

What areas of your life do you tend to lie about? What areas are you hiding? What lies are keeping you from living authentically?

_____

_____

_____

_____

_____

_____

_____

_____

_____

_____

_____

_____

_____

_____

_____

Secrets hold back your true nature and can change your identity and your behavior. But not today; change happens today! What is the truth about who you are? What do you want people to see or know about you?

_____

_____

_____

_____

_____

_____

_____

_____

_____

_____

_____

_____

_____

_____

_____

Scriptures for prayer, meditation,
and journaling your thoughts
•••••

"Dear children, let us not love with words or speech but with actions and in truth" (1 John 3:18, NIV).

_____

_____

_____

_____

_____

_____

"Do your best to present yourself to God as one approved, a worker who does not need to be ashamed and who correctly handles the word of truth" (2 Timothy 2:15, NIV).

_____

_____

_____

_____

_____

_____

"Stand firm then, with the belt of truth buckled around your waist, with the breastplate of righteousness in place" (Ephesians 6:14, NIV).

_____

_____

_____

_____

_____

"Then you will know the truth, and the truth will set you free" (John 8:32, NIV).

_____

_____

_____

_____

_____

_____

_____

"The LORD detests lying lips, but he delights in people who are trustworthy" (Proverbs 12:22, NIV).

_____

_____

_____

_____

_____

_____

"If we confess our sins, he is faithful and just and will forgive us our sins and purify us from all unrighteousness" (1 John 1:9, NIV).

_____

_____

_____

_____

_____

_____

Let's pray . . .

Father, thank you for your love in sharing the truth with me. Today, I confess that I have been lying in the areas of _____. The reason why I lie is because _____. I thank you that truth is my awareness, and it gives me access to freedom and closer relationship with You! I thank you that truth allows me to be authentically me, nothing missing and nothing added. I now know that truth is love—love for God and love for self. I declare that I am truth, and I live in truth each day in Jesus' name. Amen.

I AM TRUTHFUL!

"Like a puzzle that fits together, when you breathe through the process, you will see how all the pieces fit together to make your life an extraordinary masterpiece."

DAY
14

BREATHE!

You have received 13 words of instruction that will position you to become. Becoming the woman you desire to be isn't an overnight process but rather a step by step intentional process.

So, today, breathe!

Take in all of the words you received over the last 13 days.

Identify which of the word(s) highlight (come to the surface of your mind) for you.

_____

_____

_____

_____

_____

Which one of the words is a little more challenging to work through? No worries. Breathe, stick with it, and know that it is a process.

_____

_____

_____

_____

_____

Which one of the words brings a sense of joy?

_____

_____

_____

_____

_____

_____

_____

Which one of the words do you feel you need to review once again?

_____

_____

_____

_____

_____

Which one of the words did you find you had to refer back to when you stepped into real life situations? What was the outcome?

_____

_____

_____

_____

_____

Allow the words to align in your spirit, so you can become the woman created after God's heart!

THE ART OF BECOMING

Like a puzzle that fits together, when you breathe through the process, you will see how all the pieces fit together to make your life an extraordinary masterpiece.

Ecclesiastes 9:11 says, "The race was not designed for the swift, but for the one that is able to endure to the end."

_____

_____

_____

_____

_____

_____

Isaiah 40:8 says, "The grass may wither and the flowers fall but the word of our God endures forever."

_____

_____

_____

_____

_____

_____

Take three deep breaths in. 1, 2, and now 3. As you are doing it, think about your journey and the 13 days of the work you have completed.

Bravo!

Now, celebrate you!

"Becoming new requires your active,

daily participation of stepping

into new habits that support

and celebrate who you are."

DAY
15

Become
NEW

You are not what others say you are! As women, it is easy to take on the identity and expectations of our parents, significant others, spouses, and friends. Although they sometimes desire the best for us, their decisions for us contain what is best for them. They want to reap the benefits of what they think we can become. But deep inside, we suffer the pain because that's not who we want to be.

When we think about creating our lives, we can sometimes think about making others proud, rather than making ourselves proud. Are you going back to school because of someone else? Are you selecting that career because of your parents? Are you following family traditions because of a sense of obligation? Are you in a job you don't like because you don't want to disappoint your spouse or your friend? Are you staying in a relationship because you don't want the other person to feel bad?

You will not be perfect; you will still have your flaws, make mistakes, and be disappointed at times, but you will make your own decisions and choices! Your journey is not about perfection but about discovery. You will make decisions that will align with your likes and dislikes and not someone else's. You will also make choices that will not work in your favor, but it will still be your choice that you can learn from for your future.

Decide what choice that will be for you. Will you be confident, successful, loving, or caring but just a little sassy? Will you dance in the rain, sing your song, take an art class, meet new people, travel the world, start your own business, write a book, or change your hair color? Will you? Will you do something new? Will you dream your dream? Will you take a step for you? Will you?

When you have lived by the restraints and expectations of others, it can sometimes be a little hard to make decisions for yourself. Becoming new will require you to set some new boundaries and habits for yourself. When you have taken on everyone's expectations for you, it will take time for you to shed their expectations, so you can rise in your true nature.

I had the opportunity to speak to a woman who was married for over 20 years, but during those years of marriage, her identity and purpose were stifled by her husband's expectations of her. After going through counseling, her husband admitted that he didn't love her although she gave her very best. After giving her best and experiencing severe emotional abuse, she felt herself dying in the relationship. She came to a crossroads of continuing to choose him or choosing herself. After a long period of counseling and no change, she chose herself. Even though the relationship ended in divorce, she is in the process of learning who she is. She has to intentionally break free from the old traditions, thinking, and nature of doing things. She had to learn not to be available to him after the divorce. She had to create a new routine with herself and the children. Every day, she has to take steps towards discovering who she is with new disciplines and habits.

When you make the decision to become, it's time for you to take the action necessary to give yourself the space to become. Becoming new requires your active, daily participation of stepping into new habits that support and celebrate who you are.

When you don't become new, the "old you" will continue to make decisions on your behalf concerning your future.

Scriptures for prayer, meditation, and journaling your thoughts

•••••

"Therefore if any man be in Christ, he is a new creature: old things are passed away; behold, all things are become new" (2 Corinthians 5:17, KJV).

"For behold, I create new heavens and a new earth; and the former shall not be remembered nor come to mind" (Isaiah 65:17, KJV).

I AM NEW!

Becoming Affirmations

I love myself.

I honor myself and my purpose which is a gift

given to me by God.

I am most comfortable when

I am being myself.

I appreciate all that I am and all that I have.

I am stronger than I think.

I am patient with myself and accept the

change that's taken place within me.

"Being a fragrant woman, you are not

impacted by your external world because of

what is harnessed within.

What a fragrant woman carries is

far more valuable than

the experiences she encounters."

DAY
16

Become
FRAGRANT

W hat is your favorite scent? What fragrance are you releasing in the environments you enter?

How do you feel when you smell something that is fragrant? It changes your mood and thoughts. Having a fragrant smell can be relaxing and peaceful. When I get a massage at the spa, I oftentimes request an aromatherapy massage. I can smell the scents of lavender, eucalyptus, peppermint, rosemary, and warm vanilla. The right fragrances can have a very calming effect.

As women, when we enter any environment, we should have a sweet, fragrant smell that changes environments. The fragrant woman walks in peace, humility, confidence, courage, victory, love, and more. When a fragrant woman enters the room, she infuses the environment, situation, and the person by releasing these attributes.

Being a fragrant woman, you are not impacted by your external world because of what is harnessed within. What you carry is far more valuable than the experiences you encounters.

"True humility is staying teachable, regardless of how much you already know."

The key to being fragrant is having humility. Humility is the virtue that allows a person to admit that they cannot do it alone. It's saying, "I can't be a parent, wife, friend, business owner, student, or Fortune 500 CEO alone. I can't do it alone." Even Even with all of your education, you still must admit you don't know everything!

When you acknowledge that you can't always see where God is leading you, you leave room for Him to lead you. It's knowing that you don't always make the best decisions and sometimes even make foolish ones from time to time. It's knowing that you don't have all the answers. It's knowing that you don't always know how to withstand temptations or the outcomes. It's knowing that you don't always know how to survive the attacks of your critics. It's acknowledging that you have weak moments.

Guess what... this is all normal! It's called humanity.

This is why our humanity requires the fragrance of humility. Humility gives you access to God's grace, love, and wisdom.

When you are humble, it is a sign of your flexibility and teachability. Humility says, "I acknowledge I don't know, but I am willing to learn." It's your ability to be humble that allows you to grow in grace, peace, confidence, courage, victory, love, and so much more. Humility parts the way for God to use you, despite your flaws.

Just how does God use us despite our humanity? Let's take a look at Luke 7:37-38.

"And there was a woman in the city who was a sinner; and when she learned that He was reclining at the table in the Pharisee's house, she brought an alabaster vial of perfume, and standing behind Him at His feet, weeping, she began to wet His feet with her tears, and kept wiping them with the hair of her head, and kissing His feet and anointing them with the perfume."

For the woman to be able to wash Jesus' feet with her tears and wipe them with her hair, she had to have her head near His feet. She had to bow down with her face to the ground. Her actions illustrated a lowly and meek position that reflected humility.

She experienced brokenness because of her former lifestyle, and then she humbly accepted forgiveness for her sins and desired a new relationship with Jesus. Jesus found pleasure in both the presence and the actions of this woman at His feet. He experienced the fragrance of humility exuding from her.

The costly perfume poured out from the vial represented the woman's life savings. She was willing to give her all in gratitude to the Man who had forgiven her sins. At one point in her life, she may have been proud, but now she was humble because she had been set free from her former sinful life.

When we are not fragrant, it is because of unforgiveness, hurt, and pain of the past. There is an old saying: "Hurt people hurt other people." When you are not humble, you remain in your own thoughts, feelings, and recycled strategies—getting angrier and angrier because you are not getting results. In cases like these, your fragrance becomes a stench. Rather than drawing people to you and creating change, you repel people and provide discomfort.

There is a sacred fragrance to humility that is transmitted through a person's life in a unique way. It also reminds us that we need to be emptied or forgiven of our sins. All these efforts reflect humility in action, and they have a pleasing aroma to God.

The fragrance of humility is released and evident as a result of your speech and your behavior, so allow your speech and behavior to be pure and aromatic.

When you become fragrant, you capture the heart of God and the heart of those God allows you to come in contact with. How fragrant are you?

What fragrance are you releasing when you walk into a room? (e.g., fear, insecurities, confidence, peace, etc.)

_____

_____

_____

_____

_____

What smell are you giving off when you are having a conversation with your friends? (Ask this question of your friends or those closest to you, so you can see yourself from another perspective.)

_____

_____

_____

_____

_____

Are you still hurt by your past or have anger against someone? Does this affect your fragrance?

_____

_____

_____

_____

_____

_____

What fragrance do you release in the workplace? (e.g., joy, peace, gratitude, anger, control, etc.)

_____

_____

_____

_____

_____

_____

What fragrance do you release with your spouse, children, and family? (e.g., joy peace, gratitude, anger, control, etc.)

_____

_____

_____

_____

_____

Do you have a different fragrance with different people or is your fragrance always the same?

_____

_____

_____

_____

_____

_____

_____

Are you still attached to your former sins and pain?

_____

_____

_____

_____

_____

_____

Are you still trying to defend what God has forgiven? Is this hindering your faith and your total surrender to God?

_____

_____

_____

_____

_____

_____

Scriptures for prayer, meditation, and journaling your thoughts

•••••

"But He gives us more grace. That is why Scripture says: "God opposes the proud but shows favor to the humble" (James 4:6, NIV).

_____

_____

_____

_____

_____

"Put on therefore, as the elect of God, holy and beloved, bowels of mercies, kindness, humbleness of mind, meekness, longsuffering" (Colossians 3:12, KJV).

_____

_____

_____

_____

_____

"Do nothing out of selfish ambition or vain conceit. Rather, in humility value others above yourselves" (Philippians 2:3, NIV).

"Who, being in very nature God, did not consider equality with God something to be used to his own advantage; rather, he made himself nothing by taking the very nature of a servant, being made in human likeness. And being found in appearance as a man, he humbled himself by becoming obedient to death—even death on a cross!" (Philippians 2:6-8, NIV).

I AM BEAUTIFULLY FRAGRANT!

Becoming Affirmations

I believe in myself.

I deserve the best because I am the best.

I am becoming a better version
of myself daily.

I am grateful for every lesson that I learn.

I maintain a positive attitude because I have
what it takes to succeed.

My challenges are opportunities for me to
grow and improve.

"God gives you power in every situation,

and He gives you all power over your

enemies! You are far from being weak.

You have been built strong

through the power of God."

DAY
17

Become
POWERFUL

Your power is locked in your perspective. If your perspective is through the lens of defeat, then you will approach your situation from a victim's mentality—diffusing your own ability. However, if you see your situation from a victor's mindset, you will see opportunities to demonstrate your power.

Perspective is important when it comes to seeing your life, experiences, people, and the various challenges you may face. How you interpret a situation can make all the difference in how you react and respond.

When we face certain transitions in life, like new relationships, divorce, bankruptcy, health issues, relocation, relationship conflict, court decisions, unexpected crisis, new opportunities, job loss, or broken relationships, we can sometimes lose our sense of direction. We can sometimes question who we are and if we are capable of going through the experience.

I'm here to tell you that you are capable! You can find your position of power. Your power first comes from inviting God into your situation. When you allow Him to, He brings wisdom, strength, strategies, and understanding.

Your power comes from having a new perspective. We cannot always depend on ourselves or others to give us the insight we need. When we surrender ourselves to seeing our situation through the lens of how God and like-minded people see it, He will give you the mental strength, courage, and insight you need. Your power is displayed and illustrated when you are able to rise above your emotions, others' opinions, what's familiar, and what you naturally see to reach for faith.

God gives you power in every situation, and He gives you all power over your enemies! You are far from being weak. You have been built strong through the power of God, So, today, walk in your power by seeing yourself and your situation through the eyes and mindset of God. Always remember that every challenge you go through and endure increases your power and draws you closer to God.

After having long, knockdown fights with rejection, I had to learn how to walk in my power with practicality and skill. Here are some of the practical ways I learned to do so after understanding God's principles of power.

- **Take responsibility for your actions** – Recognize when you are wrong and take ownership. When you own it and do not deny or hide it, you will have the power to change it. That's power!

- **Apologizing** – When you have wronged someone, be quick to apologize and say that you are sorry. After you say you're sorry, be prepared to change your behavior so that your apology builds trust. That's power!

- **Don't lie** – When you lie, it weakens your character and your defense. Lying will keep you looking over your shoulder and in fear. Remain in truth and you will remain in power.

- **Don't say "yes" when you mean "no"** – Having a "yes" as an automatic response will stifle you. It will obligate you for responsibilities and tasks that you didn't sign up for. Internally, this will frustrate you and cause you to be angry with yourself and others. Always create space in between your responses and check your calendar to verify your availability. That's power!

- **Install boundaries** – Living your life without boundaries is like having no doors or windows on your house. Imagine everything and everyone having access to your home, belongings, and hard-earned possessions. Having the proper boundaries in your life will help you maintain control, leverage, and protection for you and all that you will accomplish. That's power!

- **Comparison** – When you compare yourself to others, thinking that they are better than you, you will weaken your identity and lose sight of your abilities. Understanding who you are and celebrating your abilities, talents, and strengths will keep you anchored in the power of who you are.

- **Invest in yourself** – Don't invest your time, energy, and money in others and not in yourself. Always give yourself the best because you deserve the best. Take good care of yourself by investing in your health, mind, body, and spirit. The more you take care of yourself, the better you can take care of others.

- **Excellence is key** – Whatever you do, always do it to the best of your ability, always leading, displaying, and executing in excellence. Your excellence becomes a characteristic of your power.

- **Procrastination** – Delayed obedience is called procrastination. The continual pushing off of a task or responsibility until the last minute causes stress, fatigue, and unnecessary pressure and will weaken and drain your power.

- **Forgiveness** – When you operate in forgiveness, it's a strategy to help you move through life free from negative emotions. Forgiveness is the tool you use that you can access at any time to diffuse any negative emotions of others or yourself. Forgiveness keeps you free and in your position of power.

Scriptures for prayer, meditation, and journaling your thoughts

•••••

"Behold, I give unto you power to tread on serpents and scorpions, and over all the power of the enemy: and nothing shall by any means hurt you" (Luke 10:19, KJV).

_____

_____

_____

_____

_____

"I also pray that you will understand the incredible greatness of God's power for us who believe him. This is the same mighty power" (Ephesians 1:19, NLT).

_____

_____

_____

_____

_____

_____

"Finally, be strong in the Lord and in his mighty power" (Ephesians 6:10, NIV).

_____

_____

_____

_____

_____

"But he said to me, "My grace is sufficient for you, for my power is made perfect in weakness. Therefore I will boast all the more gladly about my weaknesses, so that Christ's power may rest on me. That is why, for Christ's sake, I delight in weaknesses, in insults, in hardships, in persecutions, in difficulties. For when I am weak, then I am strong" (2 Corinthians 12:9-10, NIV).

_____

_____

_____

_____

_____

_____

"I pray that out of his glorious riches he may strengthen you with power through his Spirit in your inner being" (Ephesians 3:16, NIV).

_____

_____

_____

_____

_____

_____

I AM POWERFUL!

Becoming Affirmations

I love myself.

I make a difference by showing up and being the best I can be.

I embrace challenges and obstacles because they are designed to help me learn and grow.

I am overflowing in renewed confidence every day.

I release my attachments to anything that don't serve me! Bye Bye!

I refuse to allow anything or anyone to hold me back, I deserve to live my best life.

"When you are gentle, your character is consistent, reliable, and steady. You are aware of the needs of the people around you and willing to bring your peaceful nature into the experience."

DAY
18

Become GENTLE

" A gentle answer turns away wrath, but a harsh word stirs up anger" (Proverbs 15:1, NIV).

The gentle person attracts the trust of others because of this strength.

There is something powerful in being gentle to yourself and others. Life teaches us to become rough and hard, desensitized to who we are and our natural way of being, which is actually very tender, delicate, and gentle. We can become harsh and angry in our tone when we feel as though we are not getting our way, when we are not understood, when we are wrongfully accused or judged, or when we feel ashamed or disrespected.

Why defend who you are not? If you don't believe what others are saying, or if it's not true, why get angry and exchange harsh words?

When you understand, develop, and practice what gentleness feels like, anything that is not gentle really stands out. Why allow anger to ruin your character when gentleness can exonerate you?

When you are gentle, your character is consistent, reliable, and steady. You are aware of the needs of the people around you, and you are willing to bring your peaceful nature into the experience. Being gentle allows you to function independently of your emotions.

When you operate in gentleness, it enables you to see what kind and loving feels like and what it does not. When you are able to recognize the difference, it gives you the ability to say "no" to what disrupts or contradicts your feelings, values, morals, or what you feel or believe. Gentleness is the tool that allows you to interact in ways that are less judgmental and critical but more caring and considerate of yourself and others when it comes to your choices, actions, and communication.

Steps to Becoming Gentle

1. Stay aware of your feelings – Be honest about your feelings and don't sugarcoat what is true. If you are feeling angry, acknowledge that you are angry. If you are feeling disappointed, acknowledge that you are disappointed. Pretending that you are not feeling what you are feeling will not change the outcome or cause the situation to go away; it will only push below the

surface. Side Note: Pushing your feelings below the surface only creates further emotional destruction because compiled emotions will erupt when you least expect it.

Know that what you feel is not right or wrong, but it IS true. Acknowledging your truth allows you to become honest with yourself.

Ask yourself how you are really feeling about what is happening. It may take a while to break through the surface. You can find the answer in all sorts of places. How is your body responding? Are you tense? Are you stressed? Sick? What is your body telling you about how you feel in your mind?

2. Press pause – Create space (pause) in between the what happened and your response. Remember that everything doesn't require your immediate response. Being reactionary pulls you in emotionally without having the proper response. When you pause before you respond, it allows you to take a step back to re-evaluate the situation, own your responsibility, and then decide the appropriate response while maintaining emotional control. Putting a pause in between the situation and your response disarms others from pushing your buttons or controlling your response!

3. Connect and care – It's easy to switch your heart off so you don't feel. However, switching your heart off doesn't protect

your feelings. You can get to this point when you feel hopeless, let down, and disconnected from people or your dreams. When you're not vulnerable and making emotional investments, it will leave you feeling resentful because you're stockpiling negative emotions. Make an effort to be connected and care about yourself and others when it comes to solutions, hopes, dreams, and the future.

4. Positive investment – Being gentle doesn't seem worth it at times. However, when you choose to be gentle, it requires your personal investment. Your investment is not just for the other person but for you as well. When taking the time to exercise gentleness, ask yourself the following: Why does this situation matter? Why is this person important?

When you are gentle, you find a reason to say, "Yes, this is worth my attention and investment."

Gentleness gives you access to vulnerability, meaning, and purpose. Being gentle is the first important step that takes us from a way of life that has conditioned us to be hard and tough and shut off from our heart to one that allows us to reconnect to who we are.

Gentleness also includes self-care, which means taking care of you mind, body, and spirit. Be gentle with the words you speak and how you treat of yourself. Don't be kind to others more than you are kind to yourself.

Gentleness requires your action and participation.

Which one of the four steps above is most important for you to incorporate as you move towards being gentler in nature?

_____

_____

_____

_____

_____

What was one key point that resonated with you when reading about becoming gentle?

_____

_____

_____

_____

_____

_____

How can becoming gentle personally help you on your journey as a woman?

_____

_____

_____

_____

_____

_____

In what ways can you be gentle to yourself?

_____

_____

_____

_____

_____

_____

Scriptures for prayer, meditation, and journaling your thoughts

•••••

"Let your gentleness be evident to all. The Lord is near" (Philippians 4:5, NIV).

_____

_____

_____

_____

_____

_____

"A gentle answer turns away wrath, but a harsh word stirs up anger" (Proverbs 15:1, NIV).

_____

_____

_____

_____

_____

_____

"Be wise in the way you act toward outsiders; make the most of every opportunity. Let your conversation be always full of grace, seasoned with salt, so that you may know how to answer everyone" (Colossians 4:5-6, NIV).

_____

_____

_____

_____

_____

"But the fruit of the Spirit is love, joy, peace, forbearance, kindness, goodness, faithfulness, gentleness and self-control. Against such things there is no law" (Galatians 5:22-23, NIV).

_____

_____

_____

_____

_____

_____

I AM GENTLE!

Becoming Affirmations

I believe in myself.

I am committed to giving myself the best life.

I love myself and treat myself with kindness.

I stand up for myself.

I am capable of doing great things.

I am courageous and I stand up for myself.

"Become the you that God called you to be and not who your past says you are. Through the Word of God, we are given everything that we need to demolish strongholds, judgements, or false beliefs."

DAY
19

Become
YOU

A nd the journey continues!

Don't allow the world, your experiences, or people to redefine you. There is a gap that exists between intellectually knowing these truths about who God says we are and living them out. We cannot afford to settle for less than who we have been created to be.

We have been blessed with every spiritual blessing; we have been chosen, adopted, redeemed, forgiven, grace-lavished, and unconditionally loved and accepted. We are pure, blameless, and forgiven. We have received the hope of spending eternity with God. When we are in Christ, these aspects of our identity can never be altered by what we do. You are free!

The opposite of "pure and blameless" is "impure, stained, or guilty." Perhaps you had a life experience that caused you to feel impure, so you believe God sees you this way. You then create and live out of an identity based on your actions that is contrary to how God sees you. Take some time to grieve over the experience and invite God into your place of brokenness. After you have surrendered the lie over to God, pray that He will help you believe the truth about who He says you are and make you aware of the times you are not believing it. Then, make the choice to believe it!

One day, a young lady came to me crying uncontrollably. As her tears flowed and she gasped for breath, she tried to share with me what was bothering her. Before she spoke, I stopped her and I prayed. I prayed for God's love, peace, and comfort to touch her heart, so she could gather her emotions and thoughts to express herself. She went on to say that she had stepped outside of her marriage and slept with another man and she felt horrible. She screamed, "I have sinned, and I feel ashamed and embarrassed!"

She went on to explain more about the situation. In that very moment, I realized that her heart was surrendered and she was remorseful. Even though her actions were wrong, it still didn't redefine who she is.

How do you find you and your power when your actions are wrong?

First, being in a place of vulnerability and brokenness gave her the opportunity to invite God in to love her for who she is. God doesn't see her for her actions but sees her for who He created her to be. His love creates freedom for her to forgive herself and understand the reason she made that decision. His unconditional love allows her to examine her choices without condemnation. This process of discovery moves her beyond the shame, guilt, embarrassment, and fear so she can uncover the reasons for her actions, so she can change and not repeat the same behavior.

The process is not designed to change her identity but to empower her to become more aware of her thoughts and actions going forward. Furthermore, going through the process prevents her from repeating the past or hiding in shame. Instead, it allows God to grow her into who He has called her to be.

YOUR BEHAVIOR IS NOT YOUR IDENTITY!

Become the you that God called you to be and not who your past says you are. Through the Word of God, we are given everything that we need to demolish strongholds, judgements, or false beliefs. His love and principles empower us to do so.

Discover who you are! When we define who we are, it frees us up to live in a confident and emotionally stable manner, instead of changing who we are based on others, the jobs we receive or don't receive, how we see ourselves, and all the other ways we try to define our significance. It gives us the opportunity to experience God's unconditional love for us in new and fresh ways. And it allows us to confidently and boldly grow and share His love with others.

God created you, and you should not recreate your identity. You have already been defined by God before the foundation of the world. Always live by this standard, and you will remain focused and confident. It's not about your failures, mistakes, or shortcomings but rather the love God gives you to live boldly and confidently in who you are. God knows everything about you, and His love and promises will never change concerning you, so live freely in being you.

Are there any experiences or people that have redefined who you are? If so, explain below.

_____

_____

_____

_____

_____

_____

What are some criticisms, mistakes, or judgements you've heard concerning who you are?

_____

_____

_____

_____

_____

_____

What did you learn about you from these experiences? What is true about who you are?

_____

_____

_____

_____

_____

_____

Freedom from past mistakes begins with responsibility. Is there anything you could have done (now looking back) differently?

_____

_____

_____

_____

_____

_____

Taking responsibility and accepting your role or actions is your first step to your personal freedom. When you take responsibility, it helps you become more aware, so you can move through the process more effectively.

Scriptures for prayer, meditation, and journaling your thoughts

•••••

"For though we walk in the flesh, we do not war after the flesh: for the weapons of our warfare are not carnal, but mighty through God to the pulling down of strong holds; casting down imaginations, and every high thing that exalteth itself against the knowledge of God, and bringing into captivity every thought to the obedience of Christ" (2 Corinthians 10:3-5, KJV).

_____

_____

_____

_____

_____

_____

"Even before he made the world, God loved us and chose us in Christ to be holy and without fault in his eyes" (Ephesians 1:4, NLT).

_____

_____

_____

_____

"For we are God's workmanship, created in Christ Jesus to do good works, which God prepared in advance as our way of life" (Ephesians 2:10, BSB).

"But now He has reconciled you by Christ's physical body through death to present you holy in his sight, without blemish and free from accusation" (Colossians 1:22, NIV).

"He has saved us and called us to a holy calling, not because of our works, but by His own purpose and by the grace He granted us in Christ Jesus before time eternal" (2 Timothy 1:9, BSB).

_____

_____

_____

_____

_____

_____

"That Christ may dwell in your hearts by faith; that ye, being rooted and grounded in love" (Ephesians 3:17, KJV).

_____

_____

_____

_____

_____

MY BEHAVIOR IS NOT MY IDENTITY!

I AM ME!

"Ask God to open your eyes and your ears to hear His truth concerning you. Ask Him to reveal the uniqueness of who you are and to allow it to become evident in your life."

DAY
20

Become
UNIQUE

❝ By the grace of God, I am what I am…" (1 Cor. 15:10, NIV).

When God thought about you, He thought of every single detail. God knew all the perfect gifts, talents, temperament, personality, likes, dislikes, strengths, and weaknesses to bake into you. He chose the perfect set of experiences, challenges, accomplishments, and joys for you to encounter. He chose the family, friends, community, and even enemies that you would connect to, so you can grow and be wise. God also knew the perfect day to bring you into the world and into the Kingdom. Everything has been perfectly ordained just for you! You were planned from the very beginning. You are not a mistake. You are special in God's eyes. You are unique.

Your unique circumstances, design, and personality are amazing parts of God's design of you. God created you in His image from the very start. You have been accepted by Him from the foundations of the heavens and the earth. There is no one else like you. This makes you totally unique to the world. Being unique makes you incomparable to anyone else. There is nothing else you need to add to make yourself more pleasing and acceptable to God or anyone else. You are complete and stamped with His approval and His love

Don't waste your time trying to "unbelieve" or rationalize what has already been established. You will only frustrate yourself, limit your creativity, hinder your purpose, live below your abundance, choose wrong relationships, and stifle your growth and potential. Living contrary to your uniqueness will only keep you bound in frustration. Stay clear of what others think of you and opt to accept your unique awesomeness.

Ask God to open your eyes and your ears to hear His truth concerning you. Ask Him to reveal the uniqueness of who you are and to allow it to become evident in your life. Ask God for daily, powerful reminders of your awesomeness, so you can walk confidently in your uniqueness. Ask God to allow your uniqueness to precede you at work, in ministry, other organizations, and everywhere you go. Your uniqueness grants you favor with others and with God. Your uniqueness sets you apart from the majority and opens doors of opportunity.

Become unique!

Scriptures for prayer, meditation, and journaling your thoughts

•••••

"I knew you before I formed you in your mother's womb. Before you were born, I set you apart and appointed you as my prophet to the nations" (Jeremiah 1:5, NLT).

_____

_____

_____

_____

_____

"You saw me before I was born. Every day of my life was recorded in your book. Every moment was laid out before a single day had passed" (Psalm 139:16, NLT).

_____

_____

_____

_____

_____

"Since he did not spare even his own Son, but gave him up for us all, won't he also give us everything else?" (Romans 8:32, NLT).

_____

_____

_____

_____

_____

"For we are God's handiwork, created in Christ Jesus to do good works, which God prepared in advance for us to do" (Ephesians 2:10, NIV).

_____

_____

_____

_____

_____

_____

"Everyone called by My name and created for My glory, I have formed him; indeed, I have made him" (Isaiah 43:7, HCSB).

_____

_____

_____

•

_____

_____

_____

"For He chose us in Him before the foundation of the world to be holy and blameless in His presence. In love" (Ephesians 1:4, BSB).

_____

_____

_____

_____

_____

_____

"And have put on the new self, which is being renewed in knowledge in the image of its creator" (Colossians 3:10, ESV).

_____

_____

_____

.

_____

_____

_____

I AM UNIQUE!

Becoming
Affirmations

I embrace my flaws,

knowing no one is perfect.

I let go of all negative feelings

and stories about myself

or my life and accept

all that is good.

"When you experience unforgiveness,

it will withhold your true expressions,

prevent vulnerability,

and hold you back from

genuine relationships

and fulfilling connections."

DAY
21

Become
FORGIVING

I know becoming forgiving sounds strange when you say it, it, but it is extremely important as you move through your life. How easy is it for you to walk in forgiveness?

You see, the idea of forgiveness is easy until it's your turn to do it. It's a little bit easier to support the idea until you are in the "hot seat" extending grace to someone who may have hurt, violated, sabotaged, betrayed, or lied on you. It becomes even more excruciating when it involves someone you care about or who is close to you—family, friends, leaders, yourself, or God. When you have to become forgiving and truly extend it, it becomes an entirely different level of acceptance.

Forgiveness is not easy because it contains a lot of twists and turns. Each of our stories contains layers and layers of pain and disappointment. The truth is, you have every right not to forgive those who may have hurt you. Why? In some cases, they did! However, even justifying our right not to forgive can also work against us because we are unable to live freely when we harbor grudges in our hearts. Living life through the lens of unforgiveness can cloud your judgements and your decisions. It affects how you live your life daily and how you choose your relationships.

When you experience unforgiveness, it will withhold your true expressions, prevent vulnerability, and hold you back from genuine relationships and fulfilling connections. Ultimately, unforgiveness creates counterfeit responses, carefully measured words, and managed responses.

I remember going through an experience where I was hurt by a close friend. When confronted, the person admitted that they had intentionally tried to sabotage me. I remember crying out to God and asking Him to take the pain away. I went through days of praying that I wouldn't run into the person in the grocery store, mall, or anywhere. The pain was excruciating.

Despite the reasons for her allegations against me, God clearly showed me I had unforgiveness in my heart toward her. Since the person had admitted her wrongdoing, it didn't exempt me from searching my heart. Through surrendering my heart through prayer, I was able to see that, behind unforgiveness, I was also harboring fear, doubt, lack of trust, and resentment. God used forgiveness to show me another area of my heart I had to manage, despite the wrong that had been done to me. God's love was evident in making me aware of what I couldn't see on my own. He didn't want any hidden emotions controlling my life.

God shows us in Ephesians 4:26-27, and we see how adamant He is about forgiving ourselves and others. There are two truths: 1) unforgiveness is a sin and 2) it opens the door to the enemy. Holding on to an offense is like giving the enemy the key to our hearts. We grant the enemy unlimited access to our hearts. We grant the enemy unlimited access to our hearts to ruin our lives.

No thank you!

Now that you have a better picture of how unforgiveness operates in your life, it compels you to become forgiving and to forgive quickly. When you make this a lifestyle, you create freedom and clarity in your life. So, embrace forgiveness so nothing hinders your ability to live authentically while pleasing God. Forgiveness is an everyday choice that you choose to make.

Scriptures for prayer, meditation, and journaling your thoughts

•••••

"In your anger do not sin: Do not let the sun go down while you are still angry, and do not give the devil a foothold" (Ephesians 4:26-27, NIV).

_____

_____

_____

_____

_____

_____

"For if you forgive men their trespasses, your heavenly Father will also forgive you. But if you do not forgive men their trespasses, neither will your Father forgive your trespasses" (Matthew 6:14-15, ESV).

_____

_____

_____

_____

_____

_____

"And whenever you stand praying, forgive, if you have anything against anyone, so that your Father also who is in heaven may forgive you your trespasses" (Mark 11:25, ESV).

_____

_____

_____

_____

_____

"Judge not, and you shall not be judged; condemn not, and you shall not be condemned; forgive, and you will be forgiven" (Luke 6:37, ESV).

_____

_____

_____

_____

_____

"He has delivered us from the power of darkness and conveyed us into the kingdom of the Son of His love, in whom we have redemption through His blood, the forgiveness of sins" (Colossians 1:13-14, NKJV).

"If we confess our sins, He is faithful and just to forgive us our sins and to cleanse us from all unrighteousness" (1 John 1:9, KJV).

I AM FORGIVING!

Becoming Affirmations

I love myself.

I go confidently in the direction

of my dreams.

My self esteem and self images

grows bigger every day.

"When you experience unforgiveness,

it will withhold your true expressions,

prevent vulnerability,

and hold you back from

genuine relationships

and fulfilling connections."

DAY
22

Become
APPROACHABLE

When you go through life's ups and downs such as divorce, bankruptcy, loss of a child, failed business, broken relationships, or health issues, it can sometimes result in pain, anger, bitterness, confusion, and more unresolved issues. When we don't properly resolve our feelings, it can have a drastic effect on the relationships around us. These relationships such as those we engage in within the workplace, church, business, and friendships can be affected by unresolved emotions. Unchecked or unprocessed emotions can result in having a short temper, being sarcastic, being unforgiving, being standoffish, and having uncontrolled anger. All these behaviors result in being unapproachable.

Your unresolved emotions can get in the way of your relationships without you recognizing it. The longer you function in unprocessed emotions, the more it becomes a part of you. This becomes the plan to make you unapproachable. If you don't recognize it, you may find yourself alone and feeling rejected and misunderstood. The trick of the enemy is to have you remain in your unresolved and unchecked emotions so that, eventually, the people around you separate themselves from you—ultimately making you feel as though you are alone and unloved.

What we fail to realize is that when we go through challenging seasons of our lives, it doesn't happen to us alone. Difficult and emotionally challenging seasons happen to everyone. Just imagine if everyone held tight to their negative experiences or emotions. We would not have any people to connect with. We would actually repel each other. No one wants to be around a negative, bitter, or angry person. This is why it is extremely important that we process our feelings through the principles of God when people have wronged or hurt us. His love and principles will aid in your healing, understanding, forgiveness, peace, faith, and hope. We need these components to have healthy, productive relationships.

A young lady that I mentored grew up in a very hostile and angry environment. As a young girl, she went through lots of emotional and physical abuse, which left her no other choice but to protect herself. Her way of protecting herself was using harsh, sharp words. However, little did she know that her way of protecting herself was sending an alternative message to others that she was unapproachable and intimidating. For such a long time, she couldn't understand why she didn't have friends or why friends wouldn't stay around her for long.

It was not until she began to understand God's principles and reflect upon her actions and the effect they were having on others that she decided to trust God. In trusting God, she slowly began to let her guard and defenses down in order to receive love from God and others. As a result, she has become approachable and now has created healthy relationships.

Being approachable begins with having a healed heart. Having a heart that is forgiving creates connection. Connection is the key to being approachable. Being a person who is approachable is essential to spreading the love and peace that God gives us, so we can give it to others. If love is broken in our hearts, we have nothing to use to connect with others.

It is truly a process that is intentionally practiced every day. God desires that you show yourself as friendly, so others can experience who He is through you!

So, just how approachable are you? Let's take some action by responding to the following questions.

Do you have a heart that is forgiving?

_____

_____

_____

_____

_____

_____

Do you have a smile that is able to attract others?

_____

_____

_____

_____

_____

Do you have a heart that is able to see the best in others?

_____

_____

_____

_____

_____

_____

Scriptures for prayer, meditation,
and journaling your thoughts

•••••

"And walk in love, just as Christ loved us and gave himself up for us as a fragrant offering and sacrifice to God" (Ephesians 5:2, NIV).

_____

_____

_____

_____

_____

"May be able to comprehend with all saints what is the breadth, and length, and depth, and height; And to know the love of Christ, which passes knowledge, that ye may be filled with all the fulness of God" (Ephesians 3:18-19, KJV).

_____

_____

_____

_____

_____

_____

"A friend loves at all times, and a brother is born for a time of adversity" (Proverbs 17:17, NIV).

_____

_____

_____

_____

_____

"Make no friendship with a man given to anger, nor go with a wrathful man, lest you learn his ways and entangle yourself in a snare" (Proverbs 22:24-25, ESV).

_____

_____

_____

_____

_____

"Draw near to God, and He will draw near to you. Cleanse your hands, you sinners; and purify your hearts, you double-minded" (James 4:8, NKJV).

_____

_____

_____

_____

_____

_____

"He who loves purity of heart, and whose speech is gracious, will have the king as his friend" (Proverbs 22:11, ESV).

_____

_____

_____

_____

_____

_____

I AM APPROACHABLE!

Becoming
Affirmations

Every day I am learning to love myself more.

I am grateful for the many

blessings in my life.

"God wants us to become visible! When you are visible, you have a certain level of influence and power in the world. Those with God-inspired visibility will always lead others with the character and principles of God."

DAY
23

Become
VISIBLE

This morning, in my time of devotion, in my time of devotion I read about Cornelius. In Acts 10:2, "Cornelius was an outsider, but he was a devout man—a God-fearing fellow with a God-fearing family. He consistently and generously gave to the poor, and he practiced constant prayer to God." Almost immediately, I began to think about what makes me visible. It was apparent that Cornelius got the attention of the Lord by the things he did—devout, he was God-fearing, he raised a God-fearing family, he was generous, and had a lifestyle of prayer.

When reading this, it makes you ponder: what things do I do to get God's attention? What shows up in my life as a delight and honor to God? How visible are you before God? Do you spend most of your time being visible for others?

Visible means capable of being seen; exposed to view; capable of being discovered or being seen.

From my reading, it appears that Cornelius was visible or was seen by God based on the acts he did in honor of God and not himself. (He was selfless.) You see, we can go through life working hard in our own efforts to be seen, or we can do things that honor God and, in time, are seen by others. When we do things in our own way to be seen, it excludes God and can attract the wrong people and experiences. When you become visible without God, your efforts can be based on feelings, money, people, or other factors. When you become visible through God, your efforts are done to include Him in your actions.

On the contrary, are you the person who likes to hide? Do you hide because you are afraid and unsure of what you bring? Hiding may seem safe and comfortable for you, but it stands in the way of God displaying your purpose.

God wants us to become visible! When you are visible, you have a certain level of influence and power in the world. Those with God-inspired visibility will always lead others with the character and principles of God. God-inspired visibility produces respect, honor, trust, favor, and increase in your life. So, no more hiding or doing it on your own. God desires to position you in such a way that your life will be fulfilling, purposeful, and prosperous.

Scriptures for prayer, meditation, and journaling your thoughts

•••••

"Cornelius was an outsider, but he was a devout man—a God-fearing fellow with a God-fearing family. He consistently and generously gave to the poor, and he practiced constant prayer to God" (Acts 10:2, VOICE).

_____

_____

_____

_____

_____

_____

"You are the light of the world. A city set on a hill cannot be hidden. Nor do people light a lamp and put it under a basket, but on a stand, and it gives light to all in the house. In the same way, let your light shine before others, so that they may see your good works and give glory to your Father who is in heaven" (Matthew 5:14-16, ESV).

_____

_____

_____

"The Lord detests the sacrifice of the wicked, but he delights in the prayers of the upright" (Proverbs 15:8, NLT).

"And he said to them, "Go into all the world and proclaim the gospel to the whole creation" (Mark 16:15, ESV).

"No one after lighting a lamp puts it in a cellar or under a basket, but on a stand, so that those who enter may see the light" (Luke 11:33, ESV).

_____

_____

_____

_____

_____

"But someone will say, "You have faith and I have works." Show me your faith apart from your work, and I will show you my faith from my work" (James 2:18, CSB).

_____

_____

_____

_____

_____

_____

"For the Lord takes delight in his people; he crowns the humble with victory" (Psalm 149:4, NIV).

_____

_____

_____

_____

_____

_____

I AM VISIBLE!

Becoming Affirmations

I believe in myself.

I am happy to be alive and free mentally,

emotionally, and spiritually.

I live my life through awareness

and gratitude.

My decisions and actions bring me success.

Attracting more success comes easy and

effortlessly to me.

"Meekness allows us to stay in control

while remaining in the

love of God no matter the difficulty

or opposition."

DAY
24

Become
MEEK

How do you handle yourself during a heated discussion? How do you respond when someone disagrees with you? Do you find yourself yelling, screaming, and sometimes even cursing to express your view? How do you react when no one is listening to you or understanding your point of view? Do your emotions get the best of you? Do you regret some of the things you may have said?

You can never resolve disagreements during a heated emotional exchange. During these emotional battles, no one can hear or understand. The only goal of individuals during disagreements is to be heard and valued for their point of view, and when that is ignored, both parties shut down which results in increased hurt and pain.

Meekness is the answer. Know that meekness is not weakness. People can sometimes deem meekness as becoming a doormat for people to walk over. Meekness is a quiet strength that a person possesses as a result of their trust in God.

Harshness fires people up with anger and revenge, but gentleness provides a steady calmness. Meekness allows us to be at peace, so we are not on the defense and angry with God or with others. When we are harsh, we can provoke others into anger. When this happens, we are stirring up evil in our hearts rather than bringing an atmosphere of peace and gentleness. Meekness provides a safe place for people to open up and make themselves vulnerable, so they can properly assess their actions.

It's a lie to think that we have to be loud, rough, or curt to make our voices heard. Being loud, rough, or curt is never a guarantee that others can hear you. Being an effective communicator during emotionally intense situations requires meekness. Meekness paves the way for individuals to seek first to understand before being understood. Meekness inspires patience, understanding, wisdom, peace, and hope.

When you operate in meekness you are able to yield to God's wisdom. God has something to say about every situation we experience along with a way He wants us to handle it. It takes a long time to build good and strong relationships, but it only takes a minute to tear them down.

Meekness allows us to stay in control while remaining in the love of God no matter the difficulty or opposition. Remaining in control through meekness prevents us from destroying relationships. In how many of your relationships do you desire meekness? When you apply meekness in your life, it sparks a beauty from within that others can behold.

Scriptures for prayer, meditation, and journaling your thoughts

•••••

"Blessed are the meek, for they will inherit the earth" (Matthew 5:5, NIV).

_____

_____

_____

_____

_____

_____

"Take My yoke upon you, and learn from me, for I am gentle and lowly in heart, and you will find rest for your souls" (Mark 11:29, ESV).

_____

_____

_____

_____

_____

_____

"To speak evil of no one, to avoid quarreling, to be gentle, and to show perfect courtesy toward all people" (Titus 3:2, ESV).

_____

_____

_____

_____

_____

_____

"But the meek shall inherit the land and delight themselves in abundant peace" (Psalm 37:11, ESV).

_____

_____

_____

_____

_____

_____

"Who is wise and understanding among you? By his good conduct let him show his works in meekness of wisdom" (James 3:13, ESV).

_____

_____

_____

_____

_____

"But let your adorning be the hidden person of the heart with the imperishable beauty of a gentle and quiet spirit, which in God's sight is very precious" (1 Peter 3:4, ESV).

_____

_____

_____

_____

_____

"But the fruit of the Spirit is love, joy, peace, longsuffering, gentleness, goodness, faith, meekness, temperance: against such there is no law" (Galatians 5:22-23, KJV).

_____

_____

_____

_____

_____

_____

I AM MEEK!

"God uses silence to teach us how to be disciplined, patient, wise, and understanding. When we recognize how God utilizes silence, it protects us from taking the situation personally and retaliating from our emotions."

DAY
25

Become SILENT

---

hen I speak to you about silence, it's not from the standpoint that you have to be silent but from the standpoint of choosing to. Silence is a viable option. I know that, in life, we can easily lose our voice because of traumatic, tormenting, and frightening experiences. It is apparent that these frightening experiences can condition you to be silent. In these moments, you can easily succumb to the fear of the experience and lose your voice (the ability to speak, share, comment, or express your thoughts or opinion). When you have frightening experiences happening repeatedly in your life, it's easy to lose your voice. This type of silence is not from God. God didn't give you a spirit of fear but of power, love, and a sound mind.

When you are commanded to become silent, it's not to steal your voice but instead to prompt you to be patient, to listen, and to understand. When you become silent, it requires you to listen two times more than speaking. When you choose to be silent, you are empowered to reposition yourself, so you can listen to the person's heart and not respond to their emotions. Active listening begins with silence. When you give up your right to speak and begin to listen to the heart of another, not only are you positioned to listen, but you are empowered to respond with wisdom.

God uses silence to teach us how to be disciplined, patient, wise, and understanding. When we recognize how God utilizes silence, it protects us from taking the situation personally and retaliating from our emotions. God doesn't want us to be manipulated by our emotions or by others. He wants us in control of our emotions. God desires to protect us at all costs, so when you understand and discern when to use silence, it will preserve your character, credibility, peace, joy, future, and your relationships. When we utilize silence in our lives, it will prevent us from falling into the trap of the enemy.

Being an active listener by choosing to be silent allows the other person not only to feel valuable but also to feel that what they have to share is valuable. Your ability to listen extends the invitation for them to share freely.

Being slow to speak and quick to listen is a principle that displays your maturity, strength, discipline, and power! When you apply it, you won't have to worry about any burdens of regret.

Just think, if you're always talking, how much valuable information could you be missing?

Which relationships can benefit from you being more of an active listener?

_____

_____

_____

_____

_____

What are some of the steps you can take to listen more than speak?

_____

_____

_____

_____

_____

If you listened more than you spoke, how could this improve and strengthen the relationship with your children, spouse, friends, parents, supervisor, etc.?

_____

_____

_____

_____

_____

_____

Scriptures for prayer, meditation, and journaling your thoughts

•••••

"The one who has knowledge uses words with restraint, and whoever has understanding is even-tempered. Even fools are thought wise if they keep silent, and discerning if they hold their tongues" (Proverbs 17:27-28, NIV).

_____

_____

_____

_____

_____

"a time to tear and a time to mend; a time to be silent and a time to speak" (Ecclesiastes 3:7, NIV).

_____

_____

_____

_____

_____

"My dear brothers and sisters, take note of this: Everyone should be quick to listen, slow to speak and slow to become angry" (James 1:19, NIV).

"But in your hearts revere Christ as Lord. Always be prepared to give an answer to everyone who asks you to give the reason for the hope that you have. But do this with gentleness and respect, keeping a clear conscience, so that those who speak maliciously against your good behavior in Christ may be ashamed of their slander" (1 Peter 3:15-16, NIV).

"All scripture is God-breathed and is useful for teaching, rebuking, correcting and training in righteousness" (2 Timothy 3:16, NIV).

_____

_____

_____

_____

_____

_____

I AM AN ACTIVE LISTENER!

"When you are confident, it sends a clear message that you love yourself. The love you have for yourself is based on who you are and not what you do. Your confidence in your identity and the love you have for yourself anchors you as a woman."

DAY
26

Become
CONFIDENT

---

onfidence is the firm trust and belief of acknowledging and accepting who you are! It is the self-assurance in your abilities and your qualities. It's believing in yourself more than your fears, weaknesses, and imperfections.

If you are anything like me, you may have pursued validation from those around you at some time in your life. I was so in search of approval from my friends I neglected opportunities to truly understand and discover who I was intrinsically. I depended on others' feedback about me. Needless to say, my emotions were like a thermometer going up and down. Everything others told me was based on what I did and never truly on who I was. So, I would work extra hard to receive validation and approval based on my performance. I built codependent relationships, which resulted in being emotionally drained because I could never hit the mark of people's expectations concerning me.

Confidence becomes the game-changer in how you see yourself and how you approach life and the relationships around you. Confidence is the catalyst that teaches others how to treat you. Confidence has nothing to do with perfection or performance. As women, we relieve ourselves from pressure when we realize that no one is perfect. Everyone is on the same playing field, with weaknesses and strengths assigned to each of us. As a confident woman, you acknowledge your imperfections and celebrate them. Your applause is acknowledging that you have some weaknesses, but you also have some strengths that set you apart from others. Knowing your strengths allows you to know that you are never empty-handed, and you always have qualities that you can contribute. Confidence shows up when we stop chasing perfection, approval, and validation for the sake of others.

When you are confident, it sends a clear message that you love yourself. The love you have for yourself is based on who you are and not what you do. Your confidence in your identity and the love you have for yourself anchors you as a woman. You believe in yourself more than criticisms, results, opinions, or approval! Your confidence makes loving yourself a priority and not a luxury. Recognize, develop, cultivate, and bloom where your confidence is, and you will live a life of freedom.

Growing in confidence doesn't always mean you are 100 percent confident all the time, but you are more aware of when you shrink back.

When you walk in confidence, you will experience the following:

1) Giving yourself permission to share your thoughts
2) Being unafraid to ask challenging questions
3) Saying no to others is saying yes to yourself
4) Having the courage to accept who you are
5) Having the boldness to ask for help
6) Having the ability to commit to things you enjoy
7) Using positive words in your communication
8) Being clear about your purpose and goals
9) Understanding how to create your own success
10) Focusing on the positive and leaves negative people behind
11) Making self-care a priority
12) Resisting complaining or comparing yourself to others
13) Stepping outside of your comfort zone.

When you recognize, develop, cultivate, and bloom in confidence, you will experience freedom!

In what ways can confidence change your life?

_____

_____

_____

_____

What areas of your life require you to become more confident?

_____

_____

_____

_____

_____

How does confidence keep you on track with your purpose and your dreams?

_____

_____

_____

_____

_____

Scriptures for prayer, meditation, and journaling your thoughts

•••••

"I can do all things through Him who strengthens me" (Philippians 4:13, NKJV).

_____

_____

_____

_____

_____

"For God hath not given us the spirit of fear; but of power, and of love, and of a sound mind" (2 Timothy 1:7, KJV).

_____

_____

_____

_____

_____

"I will praise You, for I am fearfully and wonderfully made; Marvelous are Your works, And that my soul knows very well" (Psalm 139:14, NKJV).

_____

_____

_____

_____

_____

_____

I AM CONFIDENT!

Becoming Affirmations

When I practice self-love,

I become more lovable.

I am becoming the person

I want to be.

I have a strong relationship

with God.

I have faith in God

and my abilities.

"When we become peaceful, we get to understand the nature of God from a closer view. There are parts of God we will fail to encounter if we are not in a state of peace."

DAY
27

Become PEACEFUL

Where can we go to get peace? Let's get real. As women, we are tasked with so many responsibilities and so many people to manage, whether it is our spouse, children, co-workers, friends, or family. It all can fall on your plate of responsibilities. When the plate gets full, it is easy to get overwhelmed and then neglect your peace. We are leaders, nurturers, problem solvers, advocates, lovers, caretakers, and so much more.

Or better yet: have you gotten into a really bad argument that included yelling, cursing, and maybe even fighting? You felt as though your feelings were being ignored and not being heard. In the moment, all you wanted to do was defend yourself, but before you knew it, anger was taking you over the edge, with no point of return.

When it comes to your peace, you can't find it in a bottle, pills, smoking, or even sex. The peace that I am talking about goes beyond your understanding. You see, the things referenced above are subject to feelings, but the peace that goes beyond your understanding comes from God. It is a peace that draws you closer to God. When you experience the peace of God, it provides you with comfort, wipes your tears, calms anger, removes your fear, refuels your energy, clears your mind, gives you instructions, renews your strength, and gives you hope. There is nothing like it, and it's free! When you pray and ask, God is faithful to give peace.

When we become peaceful, we get to understand the nature of God from a closer view. There are parts of God we will fail to encounter if we are not in a state of peace. Learning more about God unfolds like flower petals that reveal the nature of His character. When you receive a bad doctor's report, in peace you allow Him to be your Comfort; going through a broken relationship, He becomes Your Healer; worried about paying your bills, He becomes your Provider. There are many facets to God that can only be revealed when you go through various experiences, so you fully know He will give you peace.

Scriptures for prayer, meditation,
and journaling your thoughts

•••••

"And the peace of God, which surpasses all understanding, will guard your hearts and your minds in Christ Jesus" (Philippians 4:7, ESV).

_____

_____

_____

_____

_____

"Peace I leave with you; my peace I give to you. Not as the world gives do I give to you. Let not your hearts be troubled, neither let them be afraid" (John 14:27, ESV).

_____

_____

_____

_____

_____

"Let the peace of Christ rule in your hearts, since as members of one body you were called to peace. And be thankful" (Colossians 3:15, NIV).

_____

_____

_____

_____

_____

"The LORD gives strength to his people; the LORD blesses his people with peace" (Psalms 29:11, NIV).

_____

_____

_____

_____

_____

I AM PEACEFUL!

Becoming Affirmations

I am healthy, well groomed

and confident.

My inner peace matches

my outer beauty.

"Awareness is the key to understanding

your identity, breaking habits, recycling

relationships, changing careers, identifying

your purpose, eating the proper foods,

having good health, and so on."

DAY
28

Become
AWARE

---

re you aware of your actions? Are you aware of how you respond? Are you aware of your thoughts? Awareness is a powerful tool that allows you to connect to your actions, thoughts, and behaviors. Oftentimes people go through life unaware of what they say and how it impacts those around them. They are unaware of their responses or behaviors and, as a result, they continue to repeat the same behaviors and responses until they form a habit. These habits can have an impact on your relationships, goals, dreams, and personal expectations.

When we are aware, we have a better understanding of ourselves and how we respond in certain situations. As unique beings, we have the ability to experience ourselves in different ways. We are empowered to make changes and to build on our areas of strength, as well as to identify areas where we would like to make improvements.

Awareness is the key to understanding your identity, breaking habits, recycling relationships, changing careers, identifying your purpose, eating the proper foods, having good health, and so on. Awareness gives you the invitation to change and improve your life for the better. When it comes to relationships, as women, we can become unaware of our habits and drawn by our feelings. We chase the feelings of love, and we compromise who we truly are. When we chase feelings and not what truly aligns with who we are, we don't get the results we expect.

When you are aware, your awareness becomes your path to freedom, freedom to be who you are and build the life you desire. Your awareness gives you the authority to select and reject relationships. Making decisions based on your awareness creates a life of freedom and peace.

Scriptures for prayer, meditation, and journaling your thoughts

•••••

"Be alert and of sober mind. Your enemy the devil prowls around like a roaring lion looking for someone to devour. Resist him, standing firm in the faith, because you know that the family of believers throughout the world is undergoing the same kind of sufferings" (1 Peter 5:8-13, NIV).

_____

_____

_____

_____

_____

_____

"So then let us not sleep as others do, but let us be alert and sober" (1 Thessalonians 5:6, NASB).

_____

_____

_____

I AM AWARE!

Becoming Affirmations

I am in control of my own actions.

Negativity has no place in me or my life.

My challenges are opportunities to learn.

I take responsibility for who I am:

the bad and the good.

"When you walk in the power of love,

nothing or no one can stand

in your way. Love keeps you anchored

in the essence of who you are

and who you are created to be."

DAY
29

Become
LOVE

God says, "I am love!" What does it mean to become love? When you become love, you abandon your feelings and consider others before yourself. Abandoning your feelings doesn't mean you allow others to abuse or hurt you; rather, it means that you do not take things personally or take the low road in seeking revenge against others. It is giving up your right to be right, with no desire to prove yourself to others.

Are you easily offended? Do you take things personally? Can you respond with kind words when negative words are being thrown at you? Can you resist cursing or arguing with others during a heated discussion? Can you agree to disagree, even though you know you are right? These are all questions and possible experiences that will test your ability to love beyond yourself.

When you become love, it disarm the control panel of your heart. Your heart holds all the key emotions that will create a story within your thoughts. The thoughts and feelings you are experiencing will then control how you respond. I don't know about you, but I don't like to be controlled by people or my environment.

The love that we receive from God makes us complete! His love is designed to validate, affirm, build, cultivate, and strengthen who we are in Him. Who we are is designed to withstand the emotional waves that come with conflict. When conflict or challenges arise and we fear that our identity is being attacked, we automatically go into defense mode. However, if you are complete in believing God's love for you, you don't take things personally. Your ability to become love allows you to understand and consider the other person's opinion.

When you walk in the power of love, nothing or no one can stand in your way. Love keeps you anchored in the essence of who you are and who you are created to be. You become detached from others' opinions, expectations, or criticisms against you. You can hear and respond in a kind manner. When you walk in love, you maintain your power.

I remember times where I had to "hold my peace." I wasn't wrong, but I didn't have to defend myself. I had to listen to the person but not say anything. Being complete in God's love gave me the strength and discipline to walk in love and not defend myself. Walk in love and take the high road. In the end, even though the other person admitted to being wrong in their attack against me, I learned the power of love and discipline. My strength to "hold my peace" and walk in love was my protection.

Scriptures for prayer, meditation,
and journaling your thoughts

•••••

"We love because he first loved us" (1 John 4:19, NIV).

_____

_____

_____

_____

_____

_____

"Be completely humble and gentle; be patient, bearing with one another in love" (Ephesians 4:2, NIV).

_____

_____

_____

_____

_____

_____

"Above all, love each other deeply, because love covers over a multitude of sins" (1 Peter 4:8, NIV).

_____

_____

_____

_____

_____

_____

"My command is this: Love each other as I have loved you" (John 15:12, NIV).

_____

_____

_____

_____

_____

_____

"May the Lord direct your hearts into God's love and Christ's perseverance" (2 Thessalonians 3:5, NIV).

_____

_____

_____

_____

_____

I AM LOVE!

Becoming Affirmations

I love the person I am becoming.

My inner beauty shines brightly.

I am who I need to be.

I am loved.

"Each day, step into the world knowing

that you have the ability to achieve and

produce whatever you want.

When you operate in that level of faith,

you give God room to move in your life."

DAY
30

Become
FAITHFUL

❝ Now faith is the substance of things hoped for and evidence of things not seen" (Hebrew 11:1, NKJV).

How can you live without faith? Your life was created in faith. Your future will be created in faith. Everything that you did required your faith. Everything you need will require your faith. In order for you to become faith, you must understand that your faith originates in God. Faith is not connected to money, people, religion, the economy, or things; it is connected to the belief of what is to come.

Your future dreams don't exist as of yet. You may have a glimpse of it through a magazine, person, or television, but until you produce it, you have not used your faith. Creating great relationships will require your faith. To believe you can have something and then act upon it until you see it is faith. Faith is the currency you use when you want to make an exchange from heaven to earth.

What do want for your life? It will require your faith to get it. Dream, believe, and take action!

One of the events that I love to create each year is my annual "Emerging Women Event." With this event, I host up to 20 women in a beautiful luxury home. I get the opportunity to teach, cultivate, build, and of course, pamper them. It is such a wonderful experience, not just for the ladies but for me as well. However, if I didn't rely and trust faith to produce it, I would have never met nor had the opportunity to gather these women. Your faith will create opportunities and moments that fear will never get to experience.

The more you exercise your faith, the more your creativity, vision, and ideas begin to increase.

Each day, step into the world knowing that you have the ability to achieve and produce whatever you want. When you operate in that level of faith, you give God room to move in your life.

Whatever you can see, you can produce!

Design your dream life. What does it look like?

_____

_____

_____

_____

_____

_____

Scriptures for prayer, meditation, and journaling your thoughts

•••••

"Therefore I tell you, whatever you ask for in prayer, believe that you have received it, and it will be yours" (Mark 11:24, NIV).

_____

_____

_____

_____

_____

_____

"Now faith is confidence in what we hope for and assurance about what we do not see" (Hebrews 11:1, NIV).

_____

_____

_____

_____

_____

_____

"For we live by faith, not by sight" (2 Corinthians 5:7, NIV).

_____

_____

_____

_____

_____

_____

"And without faith it is impossible to please God, because anyone who comes to him must believe that he exists and that he rewards those who earnestly seek him" (Hebrews 11:6, NIV).

_____

_____

_____

_____

_____

_____

I AM FAITHFUL!

"As an Emerging Woman, you first must love God, then love yourself, and then others...just in this order! So, remember it's always... 1, 2, 3! Stay in that rhythm and you will always have the courage and commitment to be who you are and who God has called you to become!"

Summary

Congratulations!!! We made it to the end! As we arrive at the end, we must agree that this journey was a journey of faith and lots of vulnerability. The journey to becoming required your honest look at who you are so that you can move actively into new thoughts/actions based on new information received. It sobered you up so that you can expand your perspective, insight, and capacity to EMERGE!

Becoming the woman you desire to be takes work—a lot of hard work, I may add! It's not easy going into the corridors of your mind and heart to uncover things. As women, if we had a choice, we wouldn't voluntarily choose to visit those areas of our mind and heart. Now that you have put in the work, you deserve to celebrate yourself!

Now, the journey doesn't stop here. This process is an ongoing one that requires your daily participation. In addition, different experiences will pull on what you have read and learned. Even though you have seen results in five, ten, and even in twenty-five days of reading the book, your results will require your consistency.

One final thought: this book is the beginning stages of you continuing the building of who you are as a woman! If you have coached with me or attended any of my programs/events, you know there is a rhythm we live by. As an Emerging Woman, you first must love God, then love yourself, and then others... just in this order! So, remember it's always...1, 2, 3! Stay in that rhythm and you will always have the courage and commitment to be who you are and who God has called you to become!

Congratulations again on a milestone journey! I am so proud of You!

ACKNOWLEDGEMENTS

This journey to Becoming was personally just for me (or so I thought), until God chose otherwise. I would first like to thank God for the inspiration, challenge, and the growth that He pushed me through to *Become*. *The journey to become began with me, but also includes other team players, such as my husband Bryan and my children - Bryan II, Carrington, and Kayla. The role and responsibility to be the best mother and wife can't happen without them. Their love for challenging me makes me push harder, laugh, and sometimes even cry, because I don't always get it right. However, I will never trade the joys of being a wife and mother, because these keep me on my journey to Become!*

The journey continues with my Pastor Riva Tims, whom I have served for 20+ years. The journey of serving her allowed me the space to grow as a leader in ministry. Her transparent, vulnerable, and loving heart gave me the space to develop into the leader that I am today. Her ability to see the best in me built my confidence to use my voice. Her constant encouragement, teachings, trainings, support, and prayers gave me the strength to continue on this journey to *Become!*

The journey continues with my friend and Coach Varian Brandon! As a coach, she broke me down, only to build me back up stronger. Her direct, uncensored, "in your face" approach to coaching refused to allow me to shrink back or settle. When life got tough, she pushed me right back into the ring! She loves hard and has an insatiable passion and appetite to release women from the lies and stories they tell themselves. In addition, I

ACKNOWLEDGEMENTS CONTINUES

would like to thank my Women's Leadership Circle (which is a mastermind group that is an extension of Varian) who hold a space for me to just be me! We have traveled together, cried together, laughed together, eaten together, and have been challenged together by none other Varian Brandon. During one of my lowest points, you all prayed, sent me kind messages, and simply offered your love. Your contributions in my life encourage me to continue on this journey to *Become!*

The journey continues with my family, my mom, dad, sister, and brother-in-law, who support me in all that I do. My mom and dad never cease in prayer. My sister is behind the scenes, being resourceful, protective and that constant sounding boarding that provides me wisdom that keeps me on the journey to *Become!*

The journey continues with my Majestic Life Family, for all those that have trusted me to encourage and pray for them. For all volunteers that I had the opportunity to work alongside in serving. The Majestic Life Ministerial Team and Leadership team, for serving with ALL and experiencing both challenges and achievements. To all the women and clients that trusted me to pray and speak into their lives. Your life has been a treasure to me and your story a place of inspiration. Your constant drive to become a better version of yourself stretches me to create opportunities for you to EMERGE . . . this is the reason I continue on this journey to *Become.*

So THANK YOU all, and through this book, I pray that you will witness and experience the contribution that paved the way for me to *Become!*

MEET THE AUTHOR

Michele DeCaul is a Life Strategist and founder of EMERGE Life! Her passion is to teach others to do what should be the easiest thing in the world to do...and that is to be YOU!

Her passion and purpose in life is to empower women to live fully. Through the power of prayers, she gains insight, wisdom, strategies, and uncommon boldness to push women to their next level of living. She coaches women to emerge from the shadows into a life of freedom, purpose, and true authenticity. Michele challenges her clients to move beyond what's comfortable, in order to achieve and experience their heart's desire!

CONTACT THE AUTHOR

Michele DeCaul has impacted many lives through her books, keynote speeches, live events, conferences, workshops, and client coaching.

To learn more about Michele DeCaul, you can visit:
www.micheledecaul.com

If you are interested in upcoming events:

Speaking Engagement
Emerging Women Weekend Events
Self-Care Bootcamp
Group Coaching
Private Client Coaching
Prayer Development Camps

Please contact Michele DeCaul via email:
info@micheledecaul.com